Country
Quilts

COUNTRY LIVING

Country Quilts

❧ Text by

ELEANOR LEVIE
JENNIFER PLACE
MARY SEEHAFER SEARS

Hearst Books

A Division of
Sterling Publishing Co., Inc.

New York

Produced by Smallwood & Stewart, Inc., New York City
Editor: Susan E. Davis
Designer: Dirk Kaufman
Illustrations: Wendy Frost
Pattern pieces: Roberta Frauwirth

Library of Congress Cataloging-in-Publication Data
Available upon request.

10 9 8 7 6 5 4 3 2 1

Published by Hearst Books,
A Division of Sterling Publishing Co., Inc.
387 Park Avenue South, New York, N.Y. 10016

Country Living and Hearst Books are trademarks owned by
Hearst Magazines Property, Inc., in USA,
and Hearst Communications, Inc., in Canada.

Distributed in Canada by Sterling Publishing
c/o Canadian Manda Group, One Atlantic Avenue, Suite 105
Toronto, Ontario, Canada M6K 3E7
Distributed in Australia by Capricorn Link (Australia) Pty. Ltd.
P.O. Box 704, Windsor, NSW 2756 Australia

Printed in China

ISBN 1-58816-203-6

Foreword

Everyone has a quilt in his or her life. I found mine in an Iowa antiques shop back in 1972. I was admiring an old trunk; inside were several quilts. My eye fastened on a Dresden Plate Friendship quilt made in the 1920s that had obviously never been used. Its design was beautiful, and the colors looked as good as new. I bought it for $65. When I got home, I sat down to examine it more closely. Each square had a different name embroidered on it, and in the center was embroidered the story of the quilt ~ when it was started, when it was completed, and who it was for. I know everything about my quilt, because its history is written right on the fabric. Over the years, I have collected lots of antiques, but my Friendship quilt is still the most meaningful and valuable to me.

At *Country Living* magazine, we receive a lot of mail from our readers, and quilts are the subject they are most interested in. We have also had an overwhelmingly positive response to the "Quilter's Notebook" column ever since its inauguration in 1984.

With all this enthusiasm about quilts, we decided to devote a book in our *Country Living* series entirely to quilts: making them, decorating with them, and caring for them. We hope it will inspire you to make a quilt or give you some new ideas for using quilts in your decorating.

Between the covers of *Country Living's Country Quilts*, we have gathered more than ten years' worth of our favorite country quilts, and we are offering instructions and pattern pieces for making twenty of them. There are over a hundred examples of how quilts can personalize every room in the house, adding color and graphic impact to any space. Whether you are an eager quilter or have never sewn before, you will find inspiration here. I've never made a quilt myself, though I count knitting and needlepoint as two of my favorite pastimes. But this book has inspired me. I'm ready if you are!

RACHEL NEWMAN
Founding Editor,
Country Living

Introduction

I f there is one theme that runs through *Country Living* magazine, it is quilts. A quilt is homespun, touchable art, wonderful for covering a bed, draping across a bench, or hanging on a wall. There are friendly pieced quilts, fancy appliqué quilts, Victorian crazy quilts ~ each of them special. Quilts are the banners of country life, full of the many variations the country look represents.

Quilts have layers of meaning. Their beauty is not just on the surface, though their colors may be bright and the stitching fine. The real essence of quilts is in their makers ~ women (and a few men) who led hardworking lives yet took the time to quilt. Their patient stitches have withstood the test of time; the beauty and artistry of their work continue to excite us today.

No single book could capture the entire scope of quilting. *Country Living's Country Quilts* carves out a special niche by gathering together a collection of its favorite quilts. These quilts represent a wide range of styles, including some of the finest examples of quiltmaking in America. Rest assured, there is a quilt for everyone here.

We hope that looking through these pages of colorful quilts will inspire readers to take up needle and thread and create some "gentle art" of their own. Deciding which quilts to give directions for was no easy task; we have selected twenty designs, each accompanied by illustrated directions and actual-size pattern pieces. In addition, a primer called Quiltmaking Basics gives advice and reassurance every step of the way.

There are also instructions for caring for quilts, with expert advice about hanging quilts properly on the wall. Here, too, are practical tips on how to clean, repair, and store quilts. These time-honored practices will help extend the life of every quilt.

A quilt, like all art, is unique: Even in our age of computer technology and mass production, it would be impossible to duplicate precisely the thousands of delicate stitches in a single quilt. The history of quilts is like its subject ~ a rich story sewn together from thousands of scraps of folklore and mythology. New research tells us that some of the romance and legend associated with quilts may be more firmly rooted in people's hearts than in actual fact. Yet, for all its beauty, there is something secretive about a quilt. Within its many layers and hidden stitches, a little mystery resides. And long may the mystery remain.

The Honored Quilt

Quilts: The Enduring Legacy

A woman stitching a quilt one hundred years ago had little reason to suspect the work she was doing would someday have historic impact. Her intent on those busy days was to sew bed coverings to keep her family warm and, perhaps, enjoy the conviviality of an afternoon or an evening out in the company of other women. Even though other chores were always pressing and a family's needs were never quite fulfilled, women took the time to stitch. The legacy they have left in the form of beautiful quilts is a testament to their skill and ingenuity. And to the lasting value of work invested with equal parts care and craft.

Why do quilts have an enduring effect? Why do people continue to search for ways to include them in their lives? A quilt seems to have resonance, embodying more life than an ordinary bedspread or comforter. Handstitching shows that time and care went into its making. The very look of a homemade quilt seems to invest a room with soul. The quilt stands alone as a symbol of talent, love, and pride.

Simply defined, a quilt is made from three layers of cloth: a top, filler, and a backing. The process of stitching these layers together is called quilting, yet over the years the word *quilting* has come to mean the entire process of making a stitched bedcover. This is most often done with a pattern of tiny, even stitches over the whole surface. The surface can also be patterned by using different fabrics or fabric arrangements.

While quilting reached a form of high craftsmanship in Europe by the seventeenth and eighteenth centuries, the earliest American quilts were simply two solid-colored pieces of cloth bound together with fancy stitching. Known as whole-cloth quilts, they resembled today's comforters.

Turn-of-the-century quilts from the Midwest (left) are displayed on the steep mortised steps of a kitchen in Fredericksburg, Texas. In the bedroom of an Indiana log home (opposite), a Sampler quilt made by the Amish covers a Shaker reproduction bed. An antique Amish crib quilt hangs over the bed. A tulip-patterned patchwork quilt and pillows made from an old Double Wedding Ring quilt adorn the bed in a 120-year-old farm-house built by German immigrants in Texas (previous page).

A tiny garret bedroom (above) boasts a rope daybed that is covered with a quilt found in Oklahoma City thirty years ago. Its design is a Courthouse Steps variation on the popular Log Cabin pattern. (Directions for making this Log Cabin quilt are on pages 18–19.) A treasured old patchwork quilt

and a Navajo rug are right at home in the maple-paneled bedroom of a 1920s Adirondack camp on New York's Lake Placid (opposite). A tin-lined closet in the room provides dry winter storage for linens, including the quilt.

Many American quilts were quite rudimentary well into the nineteenth century. When pioneer women in rural and frontier areas couldn't find or afford wool batting, they used newspapers or corn husks. Sometimes newspaper templates, used for cutting out quilt pieces, were sewn right into the quilt along with the fabric.

Most thrifty families had a rag bag containing bits of fabric squirreled away to be reused at some point in the future. This collection may even have included prized bits of chintz or printed fabrics. Another common practice was to make a new cover for a quilt without removing the old one, the better to create a thick, warm nest. Some quilts got so thick children could not even turn over in their beds. But they were warm, and that was most important as families set up housekeeping in often spartan surroundings.

Log Cabin Quilt

DIRECTIONS

❖ **Notes:** This Log Cabin quilt is a Courthouse Steps variation, with logs added to opposite sides of the center, rather than in the standard clockwise, or counter-clockwise, sequence of pattern pieces. As in all traditional Log Cabin quilts, the center is red, symbolizing the hearth of the home around which the log walls are constructed.

Read the Quiltmaking Basics and refer to them throughout. Remember that seam allowances must be added when cutting all pieces.

❖ **Preparing Templates:** Make the following templates, and label each one as indicated: A is a 3 ¾" (9.5 cm) square for the center. All other templates are rectangular strips (logs) 1 ¼" (3.2 cm) wide and the following lengths: B and C are 3 ¾" (9.5 cm); D, E, F, and G are 6 ¼" (15.9 cm); H, I, J, and K are 8 ¾" (22.2 cm); L and M are 11 ¼" (28.6 cm).

❖ **Cutting Borders:** From Fabric 3, cut 2 strips 1 ¼" x 36" (3.2 x 91.4 cm) and 2 strips 1 ¼" x 60" (3.2 x 152.4 cm). Set these aside.

❖ **Cutting Patches:** Cut 15 of each patch, cutting A from Fabric 1; B, C, F, G, J, and K from Fabric 2; and D, E, H, I, L, and M from Fabric 3.

QUILT BLOCK

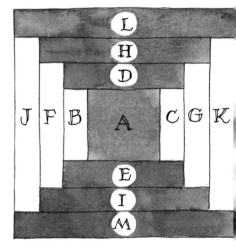

FABRIC KEY

 = FABRIC 1

 = FABRIC 2

 = FABRIC 3

ASSEMBLY DIAGRAM

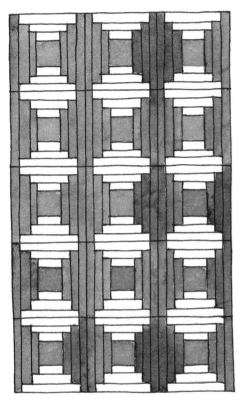

ALTERNATE ASSEMBLY DIAGRAMS

CHECKERBOARD

HORIZONTAL~VERTICAL

❖ **Making Each Block:** Refer to the quilt block diagram. Apply the patches in alphabetical order, and press the seams outward for each pair of same-color logs as you go. To begin, stitch a B and C to the opposite sides of A; press. Stitch a D and E to the top and bottom of A, plus the ends of B and C, completing a square. Stitch F and G to the opposite sides of the square, alongside previous same-color logs. Stitch H and I to the top and bottom, again completing a square. Continue in this manner, adding J, K, L, and M, to create a finished block that measures 11 ¼" (28.6 cm)

square within seam allowances. Repeat for 15 blocks.

❖ **Assembling the Quilt Top:** Referring to the Assembly Diagram, arrange the blocks in 3 rows of 5, with the same color fabrics adjacent. Or rotate the positions of some blocks to experiment with other pattern variations; 2 other possibilities are shown. Stitch the blocks together within each row; then stitch the rows together, taking care to match seams.

❖ **Making the Border:** Stitch a shorter strip to the top and the bottom of the quilt top; then trim the ends even with

the quilt top. Stitch the longer strips to the sides, trimming the ends even with the quilt top.

❖ **Assembling the Quilt:** Mark the quilt top for quilting: On the quilt shown, there is a 4-pointed compass star on each center square, with double diagonal lines over all the log patches. Cut and piece the backing. Cut the batting and baste the layers together.

❖ **Finishing:** Quilt as marked or as desired. Make a binding from Fabric 1 and attach it all around.

The years 1830 to 1900 marked a high point in the history of American quilts. Favorite motifs reflect America's unique history: the Pine Tree comes from the Colonists' earliest pine tree flag, the Log Cabin honors hearth and home, the Bear's Claw tells of westward expansion, and eagles and flags speak always of patriotism.

The majority of quilts are either pieced or appliqué. These terms are derived from the different methods of decorating the quilt top. Pieced quilts, or patchwork quilts as they are more commonly called, are made by arranging straight-sided pieces of fabric into blocks or other geometric patterns. In appliqué quilts, fabric pieces are applied to a larger cloth surface and are often shaped in floral, bird, or leaf motifs. Both patchwork and appliqué quilt tops are then combined with an inner layer of batting and a backing layer, and all three layers are quilted with decorative stitching to hold the layers together.

Traditionally, pieced quilts have been viewed as the poor cousins of appliqué quilts, though in terms of sheer artistry this is hardly so. But the myth has stuck because many of the earliest pieced American quilts were often sewn from remnants of cast-off clothing ~ old-fashioned recycling by hard-working women who tried to make the most of everything they had. Except for homespun, cloth was scarce during Colonial times; textile production was discouraged to keep the settlers dependent on British goods. Quilts of both varieties were a luxury well into the nineteenth century until New England's mills flourished. Up until then only a tiny number of wealthy women were able to purchase fabric and had the time to make elaborate quilts. So precious was fabric that even a bag of scraps had barter value.

The prints and patterns of cherished textiles brighten the back bedroom of a West Virginia farm built in the early 1800s (opposite). A tall herb-drying rack is a fitting resting place for a Rail Fence quilt that overlaps a complex Pinwheel design. A coverlet warms an old bed with acorn finials. Handwoven rugs atop the unfinished floorboards are much appreciated in winter.

The same was true of appliqué quilts well into the twentieth century. Only a limited number of women could afford the huge quantities of store-bought cloth needed for the continuous top and bottom layers and imported silks, satins, and velvets used to make elaborate designs. In fact, appliqué quilts were so highly regarded that they became status symbols in the decades following the Civil War. Even the wealthy reserved them for special occasions or set them out for show on a "guest bed."

In England and Wales, where quilts were highly valued as an art form, they were usually made by one person; asking friends for help was simply not done. They were also made by itinerant stitchers who traveled from farm to farm (in much the same way as America's itinerant painters), arriving with a quilting frame and living with a family until the job was done. Or a family could hire someone from a quilting club, whose members, paid in weekly installments, made quilts for a living. Some Englishwomen brought their own fabric and batting to be assembled by the village quilter, who was also willing to stamp a quilt top with a design that could then be finished at home.

What a far cry from these business transactions were the lively quilting bees of American folklore. Needles singing, talk aplenty, quilting bees were prime times for socializing and catching up on all the local news ~ group therapy, nineteenth-century style. Though not the custom in every community, the quilting bee was the perfect symbol of the new country, where people had to pool their resources and support each other to survive. For women with the need for companionship and artistic expression, quilts provided a ready outlet. Assembling the quilt top was often a solitary pursuit, but quilting the three layers together was frequently done in a group.

Folklore about quilting abounds. One popular myth is that every young woman hoped to make a number of quilt tops before she was betrothed. Because fabric was expensive, the tops were not sewn together with batting and backing until the marriage was felt to be a "sure thing."

In Victorian times, Crazy quilts were used as splashy parlor throws to show off their colors and stitchery. The trend still endures, as in a Massachusetts farmhouse (above) where a 1910 Pennsylvania Crazy quilt is tossed on an Indian-patterned ottoman. The backs of chairs and benches are handy display spots for quilts. The high back of an eighteenth-century Vermont settle (opposite) is decorated with special textiles that include a Log Cabin crib quilt.

One way a young lady would announce her engagement, so the story goes, was by bringing her finest finished quilt top to a quilting bee. There, everyone worked on finishing the "bride's quilt," which was usually all-white patchwork or appliqué.

American women have long spoken with their needles. And their voices are still being heard today.

Acorn Appliqué Quilt

DIRECTIONS

❖ **Notes:** Read over the Quiltmaking Basics and refer to them throughout. Remember that seam allowances must be added when cutting appliqués and all other pieces.

❖ **Cutting Backgrounds, Sashing Strips, and Borders:** Cut the following strips: from light fabric, 3 blocks 12" x 65 ½" (30.5 x 166.4 cm) for background pieces, plus 2 blocks 3" x 43 ½" (7.6 x 110.5 cm) and 2 blocks 10" x 76 ½" (25.4 x 194.3 cm) for borders. From dark fabric, cut 4 blocks 2 ½" x 65 ½" (6.4 x 166.4 cm) for vertical sashing strips and 2 blocks 2 ½" x 43 ½" (6.4 x 110.5 cm) for top and bottom sashing.

❖ **Preparing the Appliqués:** Fold an 11" (27.9 cm) square of tracing paper in half horizontally and vertically. Unfold it and place one fourth of it over the actual-size quarter-pattern shown on page 196,

THE ESSENTIALS

FINISHED SIZE

63 ½" x 76 ½" (161.3 x 194.3 cm)

·

MATERIALS

4 ⅜ yards (4.0 m) for backing

4 yards (3.7 m) light-colored fabric for background and borders (ecru is used in this quilt),
3 ½ yards (3.2 m) dark or contrast-color fabric (here, red) for appliqués, sashing, and binding

·

Sewing thread in the same contrasting color; quilting thread (optional)

·

Batting

·

Additional supplies as listed in the Quiltmaking Basics on page 185

with the fold lines of the folded square over the dash lines of the pattern. Trace the solid lines of the shape. Refold the tracing paper and cut along the solid lines, making sure to cut through all 4 layers. Unfold. Glue this to cardboard, let the glue dry, then cut the shape out. Use this template to mark 15 appliqué

One technique for designing an appliqué pattern is to cut it from folded paper, using the same method children use to cut snowflakes. Decide on the size of the repeat [here, a 10" (25.4 cm) square], and fold a same-size paper square in half horizontally, vertically, and diagonally. Cut simple designs into the folds and outer edges; then unfold the paper to view the results. This technique is often used in making Hawaiian quilts.

This quilt was, no doubt, made in mainland America, probably in the middle of the nineteenth century. While there is no way to know for sure that the quiltmaker had an acorn in mind when she designed her motif, acorns and oak leaves were often included in botanical appliqués.

motifs on dark fabric. Cut these out, leaving seam allowances all around.

❖ **Making the Appliqué Strips:** Pin 5 appliqués on each background piece, beginning 1 ¾" (4.5 cm) from the short edges and leaving 1 ½" (3.8 cm) between pieces, measuring from the seam lines of the appliqués, not the raw edges. Center each motif along the width, checking to make sure there are equal distances between the tip of each acorn in the motif and the long edge of the back-

ground piece. Appliqué each motif to the background by hand.

❖ **Assembling the Quilt Top:** Stitch the background pieces between dark vertical sashing strips. Stitch a dark sashing strip across the top and bottom. Stitch a light border strip across the top and bottom; then stitch a light border strip along each side.

❖ **Assembling the Quilt:** Mark the quilt top for quilting, if desired. Cut the

backing and the batting and baste the layers together.

❖ **Finishing:** Quilt as marked or as desired. On the quilt shown in the photograph above, there is standard quilting within each appliqué motif, contour, or echo, quilting around each motif over the background pieces, and rows of diagonal lines of quilting over the sashing and borders. Using the dark fabric, make a binding and attach it all around the quilt.

An Album quilt was created to commemorate a wedding or a young man's coming of age. It was also the gift of choice for appreciated ministers or for beloved friends who were moving away. Album quilts were often a group effort; they were signed with all the contributors' names by one especially skilled embroiderer, or each block was signed individually by its maker. Sometimes an Album quilt was made entirely by one woman. A more recent example is this embroidered Album quilt stitched by Sophia Fairfield Wheat of McLean, Virginia, who worked on it from 1965 to 1974. The patches are 10 by 12 inches. Each recounts one of the episodes in the history of the Fairfield family, which Mrs. Wheat remembered her father telling when she was a little girl. Today, her own grandchildren read the quilt to discover their roots. This is genealogy stitched with love. Closeups of some of the individual blocks are shown on the opposite page.

From Yorkshire, England

Jonas Weed landed at Watertown, Mass in 1631

N W S E

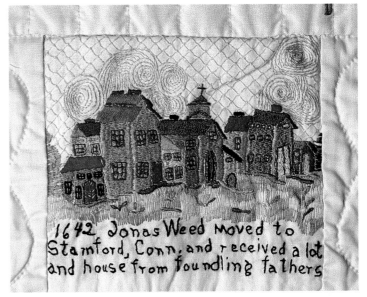

1642 Jonas Weed moved to Stamford, Conn. and received a lot and house from foundling fathers

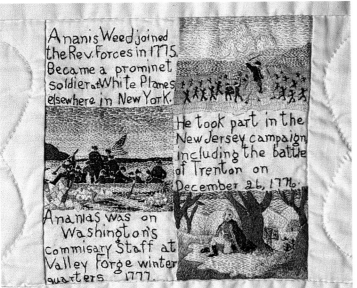

Ananis Weed joined the Rev. Forces in 1775. Became a prominet soldier at White Planes elsewhere in New York.

He took part in the New Jersey campaign, including the battle of Trenton on December 26, 1776.

Ananias was on Washington's commisary Staff at Valley Forge winter quarters 1777.

P.T. MORAN CO. 3961 FEEDS 3959

PURINA CHOWS-PRATTS and SPECIAL FEEDS FOR

HORSES-COWS-HOGS-POULTRY

HAY GRAIN STRAW FEEDS | POULTRY AND STOCK REMEDIES | FLOUR CORN MEAL MILL FEED

P.T. Moran Co 3959 M St. N.W. Washington D.C. established 1886. Owned and successfully operated by John A. Wheat, Pres. 1932-1955

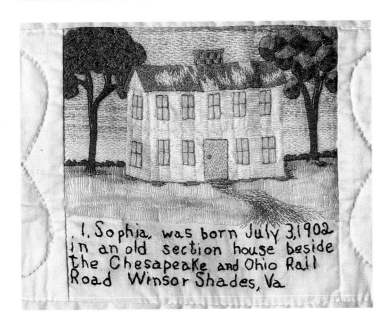

I, Sophia, was born July 3, 1902 in an old section house beside the Chesapeake and Ohio Rail Road Winsor Shades, Va.

Mina was the first girl in town to learn to drive a car. Aug. 30, 1916 she married Magnus Booth. Two daughters blessed this union. Mildred Louise born Feb. 10, 1918. Elizabeth Fairfield Sept. 20, 1920.

Living with Quilts

The sunny colors of an Orange Peel Reel quilt brighten a cool blue-and-white bedroom (above). A brown, black, and white Cross and Crown quilt made in the 1960s by the Freedom Quilting Bee cooperative in Alberta, Alabama, keeps company with an older red-and-white quilt, a variation of the same pattern (left). A red-and-white Ocean Waves quilt points up the detailing on a bed handpainted in an Old World style (opposite). Pillow covers stitched from quilt pieces rest against ruffled oxford-cloth shams. Instead of a dresser in this bedroom, an old kitchen cupboard offers just as much storage. The architectural feeling of an uncurtained tester bed is underscored by a hand-made Square-Blocks quilt with Four-Patch sashing of the owner's own design (previous page). A colorful Star of Bethlehem quilt is folded in the chair.

Beds ~ The Best Perspective

In the earliest American homes, quilts were made solely for beds. A pioneer home had no bedrooms to speak of, and a bed was often just a stack of quilts on the floor in front of the fire. If a family did own a bed, it was afforded a place of importance in the warmest room of the house, which was usually the kitchen or all-purpose great room. Making warm quilts was a necessity well into the nineteenth century in rural and frontier areas, an ongoing task as quilts wore out and newborns needed bedcovers. A woman's hands were never idle as she worked to keep her household running and her family alive. She pieced quilts ~ as many as she could turn out ~ for the long winters ahead. During the coldest nights, a family would sleep together under a thick stack of quilts to keep warm.

In many villages and towns, by the mid-eighteenth century life was somewhat easier, and beds and bedrooms more commonplace. Only when a household achieved a certain level of affluence did the family quiltmaker have the luxury of regarding her craft as more than a utilitarian enterprise.

Most of the antique quilts that survive today were made specifically for beds, so when decorating a bedroom with quilts, that is the place to start. The decorating begins the moment a quilt is spread on the bed, its center design the picture, its borders providing the frame.

A quilt spread out on a bed offers a chance to appreciate its pattern from a bird's-eye perspective. That is how its graphic mix can be truly savored. A quilt's colors, its pattern, and its fabrics set an immediate tone for a room. On a stately four-poster bed, a cherished white appliqué quilt conveys a formal air. On the other hand, a pair of colorful Nine-Patch quilts tossed on maple bunk beds ignites an entirely different kind of excitement.

A stack of quilts looks beautiful anywhere, but especially in a bedroom, on a banquette or on a bench at the foot of the bed. The array of colors and stitching patterns makes a pile of quilts a visual feast. Fold quilts so a lot of color can be seen along the fold; experiment to find just the right way of showing each off to best advantage. In a few weeks time, rearrange the quilts, making sure to refold them ~ refolding keeps the quilts from wearing along the creases. Filling a bedroom armoire with quilts and leaving the doors open is a time-honored way to display a collection.

An old general store was converted into a home, and this
is now its upstairs bedroom
(left). The appeal of the room
is due in part to its simplicity.
In the quiet surroundings,
textiles and stenciling attract
the eye. The bed, made from
a kit, is spread with a cheerful
red-and-white Diamond
Checkerboard quilt, which
is rotated with the seasons.
Overhead, the fishnet canopy
is a finishing touch that gives
the bed a bridal-like air.

The Quilter's Network

Joining a quilting group is an excellent way to pick up some of the latest ideas about quiltmaking, collecting, or decorating with quilts. Hundreds exist in all parts of the country. Most are small, ranging from informal gatherings of friends to church guilds. The New England Quilter's Group is one of the biggest with more than 1,500 members. The oldest group may be the Goodwives Quilters in Darien, Connecticut, which goes back to the 1600s, when the "good wives" of the town gave food and blankets to Native Americans in the region. The AIDS Memorial Quilt is the largest quilt project; its 10,848 commemorative panels, each 3 by 6 feet, cover 14 acres and weigh 16 tons.

Generally, larger organizations are more structured, providing classes, offering scholarships, and promoting quilt shows. The Empire Quilters hold monthly meetings in New York City that usually include a presentation of an artist's work or a lesson on a specific technique, a short business meeting, and a discussion of members' work. Many organizations, especially church groups, make quilts to raffle off for worthy causes.

One successful economic enterprise is The Freedom Quilting Bee, a cooperative founded in Alberta, Alabama, in 1966 at the height of the civil rights movement. Started by black women to raise their spirits and their incomes by selling handmade quilts, the group's continuing success has helped ensure economic independence for its members as well as a higher standard of living for their families.

For information on quilting groups in communities throughout the country, good sources are the local fabric or crafts store, the YWCA, churches, and adult-education facilities. Several very helpful national newsletters publish timely information about both traditional and contemporary quilting (see Resources on page 204).

Many organizations and institutions provide a range of resources on quilts. Among the best known is the Museum of American Folk Art in New York City, which has an 8,000-volume research library and extensive archival material. The museum sponsors The Great American Quilt Festival, with exhibits, lectures, and workshops, in New York every other May. The museum also offers a "Quilt Connection" membership, including a quarterly newsletter, for anyone interested in quilting.

The American Quilt Research Center at the Los Angeles County Museum of Art is a national repository for material on the history of quilts. In addition to more than 150 primarily American nineteenth-century quilts, the center's collection includes periodical literature (magazines and newsletters), diaries, letters, personal journals, photographs, and transcripts of oral interviews. It also houses the research files and slides of the California Heritage Quilt Project, which documents works made in or brought to California before 1945.

The American Quilt Study Group in San Francisco is a nonprofit membership organization

that promotes and publishes research on quilt and textile history. It maintains a research library of books, periodicals, and other related materials, and offers seminars and publications.

For those interested in modern quilts, The Museum of the American Quilter's Society, which opened in 1991 in Paducah, Kentucky, offers educational programs, workshops, seminars, lectures, and tours. The American Quilter's Society runs a quilts-for-sale program through its quarterly magazine. The entire city of Paducah celebrates quilting every spring with the National American Quilter's Society Quilt Show.

All these groups and institutions are helping to bring the traditions, the craft, and especially the art of quilting into the twenty-first century.

Feathered Stars Quilt

DIRECTIONS

❖ **Notes:** This quilt is constructed of 16 blocks of patchwork stars. Each star has 8 points and a sawtooth frame that gives the star its "feathered" appearance; the simple border all around serves to contain the design. Extra patience and care will be needed to produce a clean zigzag around each star.

Read the Quiltmaking Basics and refer to them throughout. Remember that seam allowances must be added when cutting all pieces.

❖ **Preparing Templates:** Refer to the diagram that shows one quarter of the quilt block. Make templates for the patches as follows: A is an 8" (20.3 cm) square; B is the triangle that results when a 3 ¼" (8.3 cm) square is cut diag-

onally in half; C is a 1" square (2.5 cm); D is the triangle that results when C is cut diagonally in half; E is the triangle that results when a 1" x 1 ⅛" (2.5 x 2.9 cm)

rectangle is cut diagonally in half; for F, trace the actual-size diamond shown on page 193; G is a 4 ¾" (12.1 cm) square; H is the triangle that results when a 7" (17.8 cm) square is cut diagonally in half.

❖ **Cutting Borders:** From the dark fabric, cut 4 border strips: 6" x 94" (15.2 x 238.8 cm). Set these aside.

❖ **Cutting Patches:** For each block (make 16), cut the following from the dark fabric: 1 A, 8 B, 4 C, 4 D, 48 E (reversing the template for half of the E patches), and 8 F. From the light fabric, cut 4 G, 4 H, 16 D, and 48 E (reversing the template for half the E patches).

❖ **Making Each Block:** Assemble the patches by following the diagram for each quarter of the quilt block as follows: First, make 48 pieced rectangular units by stitching light and dark Es together along their long edges. For each star point, join the small patches and units in rows as indicated within the heavier lines on the diagram. Stitch the shorter rows to adjacent sides of a C patch as shown and then to the short edges of 2 B patches. Stitch the longer rows of patches and units to the long edges of the B patches, ending with an F patch. Make 8 star points in all. Sew each star point to the sides of an A patch as shown, matching corners of the A square and B triangles carefully, and setting in dark D patches with the centers of the longest edges at the midpoints of each side of A. To complete the quilt block, set 4 G squares and 4 H triangles alternately between star points as shown in the diagram. The block should measure 19 ½" (49.5 cm) square within seam allowances. Make 16 quilt blocks in this way.

❖ **Assembling the Quilt Top:** Arrange the quilt blocks in 4 rows of 4. Stitch the blocks together within each row; then sew the rows together, taking care to match the seams and points of the F patches. Stitch the border strips to all sides of the quilt top, mitering the corners.

❖ **Assembling the Quilt:** Mark the quilt top for quilting if desired. As shown, the quilt features diagonal rows of quilting, running in one direction over the dark fabrics, in the opposite direction over the light fabrics. Cut and piece the backing. Cut the batting and baste the layers together.

❖ **Finishing:** Quilt as marked or as desired. Make a binding from the light fabric and attach it all around.

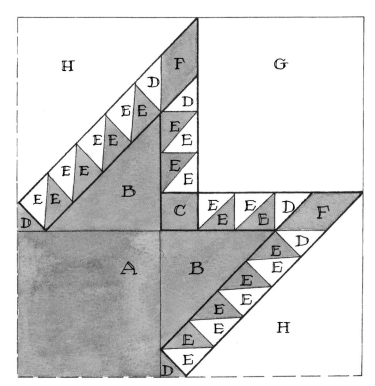

¼ QUILT BLOCK

COMPLETE QUILT BLOCK

The Dynamics of Color

Color is so powerful and provocative, it can dramatically influence the mood or tone a quilt will convey. Depending upon its colors, a quilt can look light and delicate, dark and somber, or lively and energetic. A certain color can evoke a feeling or call up favorite associations from the past.

Contrast is the most important element to consider when choosing colors for a quilt. It is what makes a pattern discernible and distinctive. Color contrast is based on the principle that light colors come forward and darker ones recede, so that a particular mix of lights and darks will have a related effect in a pattern. For instance, the same Log Cabin pattern can look like diamonds, zigzags, or stripes depending on the placement of color in it.

Varying how colors are used in a pattern is a time-honored idea. Two people stitching the same pattern using different colors can achieve markedly different results, as shown in the two Churn Dash quilts pictured here. (Directions for making the Churn Dash quilt shown on page 39 are on pages 40–41.) Other

variations are also possible, as illustrated in the diagrams.

Small areas of contrasting colors can produce optical illusions or dazzling effects that can make a quilt seem to sparkle, hop, or tumble off a wall. On the other hand, a quilt with large areas of soft color seems to blend quietly with its surroundings. The

temperature of a color (warm or cool) and its intensity (bright or dull) also contribute to the effect it creates.

When joined with color, shape also helps create movement in a quilt, leading the eye in many directions. Bow Ties and Double Axehead forms are just two of the most active patterns.

Churn Dash Quilt

DIRECTIONS

❖ **Notes:** The Churn Dash pattern is a glorified variation of the Nine-Patch. In the quilt shown, the fabrics used in the dark patches vary slightly from block to block, but all have the same background color. For simplicity, the directions refer to light- and dark-colored fabric.

Read the Quiltmaking Basics and refer to them throughout. Remember that seam allowances must be added when cutting all pieces.

❖ **Preparing Templates:** Make templates as follows: For the patches, A is a 2" (5.1 cm) square, B is the triangle that results from cutting a 4" (10.2 cm) square diagonally in half. Also make templates for the sashing pieces: C is 1¼" x 10" (3.2 x 25.4 cm), D is 1¼" x 11¼" (3.2 x 28.6 cm), and E is a 1¼" (3.2 cm) square.

❖ **Cutting Borders:** Cut the following strips: 4 strips 2" x 86" (5.1 x 218.4 cm) and 4 strips 2" x 104" (5.1 x 264.2 cm) from dark fabric for the inner and outer borders; 2 strips 2" x 86" and 2 strips

THE ESSENTIALS

FINISHED SIZE

84" x 102" (213.4 x 259.1 cm)

•

MATERIALS

5¾ yards (5.3 m) for backing

•

3¾ yards (3.4 m) of light-colored fabric, 6½ yards (5.9 m) of dark-colored fabric(s) for patches, sashing strips, and borders

•

Sewing thread to match the light fabric

•

Batting

•

Additional supplies as listed in the Quiltmaking Basics on page 185

2" x 104" from light fabric for the middle border. Set these aside.

❖ **Cutting Patches:** Use the templates to cut 200 A, 160 B, and 80 E from light fabric and 160 A, 160 B, 80 C, and 80 D from dark fabric.

❖ **Making Each Block:** Make 40 blocks in all. For Unit I (see diagram), join a light and dark B together along their longest edges. For Unit II, stitch a light and dark A together. Make 4 each of Unit I and Unit II. Arrange them around another light A patch, as shown

UNIT I   UNIT II

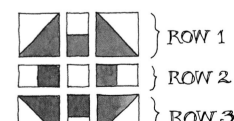

} ROW 1
} ROW 2
} ROW 3

QUILT BLOCK ASSEMBL
DIAGRAM

SASHING

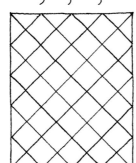

ASSEMBLY DIAGRAM

KEY

◇ = QUILT BLOCK

◁ = HALF BLOCK

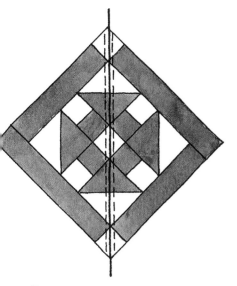

HALF BLOCKS

in the Quilt Block Assembly Diagram. Row 3 is identical to Row 1, except that it is simply turned around. Stitch the units and patches together into horizontal rows; then stitch the rows together, taking care to match the seams.

❖ **Sewing the Sashing:** Stitch a C strip to the opposite sides of the quilt block. Stitch an E patch to 1 end of 2 D strips. Following the diagram for the sashing,

arrange the D-E strips with the Es at opposite corners and stitch them to the remaining sides of the quilt block.

❖ **Making Half Blocks:** On 9 quilt blocks, draw a line diagonally down the center: On 5 of the blocks, make the diagonal line bisect the E patches, as shown in the diagram; on the remaining 4 blocks, make the diagonal go the opposite way through the ends of the D strips. On the sewing machine, stay-stitch ⅛" (0.3 cm) to either side of the marked line. Cut along the marked line to make 18 half blocks.

❖ **Assembling the Quilt Top:** Following the Assembly Diagram, arrange the blocks and half blocks on point. Keep the light E patches at the top and bottom in vertical configurations. Stitch the blocks and half blocks together in rows as shown; then stitch

the rows together, taking care to match the seams.

❖ **Adding Borders:** Stitch the shorter strips for each border to the top and bottom of the quilt, then stitch the longer strips to the sides. Begin with an inner border of dark strips, add a middle border of light strips, then finish with a dark outer border.

❖ **Assembling the Quilt:** Mark the quilt top for quilting, if desired. Piece the backing. Cut the batting and baste the layers together.

❖ **Finishing:** Quilt as marked or as desired. As shown, the quilt has straight lines bisecting each A patch diagonally, contour quilting on the B patches, and diagonal parallel lines 1" (2.5 cm) apart over all borders. Make a binding and attach it all around.

A single quilt is a fine decorating tool, as it always commands attention. To take an interesting look one step further, just increase the number of quilts in a room and combine patterns to intensify the effect. In a bedroom, spread a quilt on the bed, then add quilt "accessories": quilts draped over a chair or chaise, stacked on a table, laid on open shelves that have been wrapped with fabric, or folded in a painted cupboard. These items give a room more depth and dimension than one quilt can possibly deliver, no matter how spectacular it may be.

To successfully combine patterns in a room means becoming a matchmaker. Shapes provide clues. Bow Ties look good with Broken Dishes or with Pinwheels, because all the pieces are triangular. Other patterns built around similar simple motifs also go together well: A Nine-Patch is a natural with plain blocks, creating an Irish Chain varia-tion. The Six-Pointed Star pattern is a more elaborate version of the Baby Blocks pattern. Triangles inside triangles, facing in the same direction, make a Flock of Geese pattern. Triangles inside rectangles become the Wild Goose Chase pattern. The square block designs of One-Patch and Nine-Patch quilts make them a natural twosome.

Pairing appliqué quilts may be even easier than combining pieced quilts, because the motifs often stem from nature and blend together in cotton as well as they do in their natural state. Oak leaves, acorns, baskets of flowers, wreaths, and birds, when translated into quilts, can create a garden-like bedroom. In a child's room, a Schoolhouse pattern might be paired with a Sunbonnet Girls quilt because both echo the growing-up years. They may not match exactly, but wallpaper, a rug, or a dust ruffle that coordinates with both can be the unifying item that pulls the room together.

Beloved quilts in a number of different patterns decorate this pink-and-white guest cottage on a Michigan lake (above). Tufting adds textural interest to the pieced Star quilt on the bed. A fragment of a quilt top becomes a cushion for the wicker rocking chair. At a country inn in California (opposite), quilts, lavender walls, and lace curtains promise guests thoroughly romantic surroundings. A white Marseilles spread is topped with an Album quilt and a Nine-Patch quilt in soothing pastels. The lavender pillowcase was created by folding an embroidered dresser scarf in half and stitching it to a cloth backing. Hearts of dried rosebuds dot the wall.

Squares-in-Squares Quilt

DIRECTIONS

❖ **Notes:** This quilt has one quilt block in which the colors are reversed; the Amish and other pious quiltmakers would often include such a "devil's eye" in a quilt to ward off evil. It is more often called a "humility block" because only God can be perfect. You may want to include this reverse block in your design, or you may prefer to make all the blocks consistent.

Read the Quiltmaking Basics and refer to them throughout. Remember that seam allowances must be added when cutting all pattern pieces.

❖ **Preparing Templates:** Actual-size patterns for the quilt block are shown on page 193. Make one template each for A, B, C, and D.

❖ **Cutting Borders:** From the light fabric, cut 4 strips 3" x 28" (7.6 x 71.1 cm). Set these aside.

❖ **Cutting Patches:** For each block (make 25 for a consistent design, 24 if you are including 1 reverse block), cut 4 B and 4 D from the light fabric, 1 A and 4 C from dark fabric. For a reverse block, cut 1 A and 4 C from the light fabric, 4 B and 4 D from dark fabric.

❖ **Making Each Block:** Work outward in alphabetical order. To begin, stitch the

QUILT BLOCK

REVERSE BLOCK

long edge of each B patch to a side of the A square, forming a 2" (5.1 cm) square within the seam allowances. Stitch the long edge of each C patch to a side of the pieced square, forming a 2 $\frac{13}{16}$" (7.1 cm) square within the seam allowances. Stitch the long edge of each D patch to a side of the pieced square, forming a 4" (10.2 cm) square within seam allowances. Figures show the arrangement of patches for the quilt block and for the reverse block.

❖ **Assembling the Quilt Top:** Place the quilt blocks in 5 rows of 5. Position the optional reverse block as shown in the photograph or wherever you wish. Stitch the blocks together within the rows, taking care to match the seams at midpoint. Then stitch the rows together, matching all seams.

❖ **Making the Border:** Stitch 2 strips to either side of the quilt top. Trim the ends even with the quilt top. Stitch the

remaining strips to the top and bottom of the quilt and trim their ends even with the sides.

❖ **Assembling the Quilt:** Mark the quilt top for quilting, if desired. Cut and piece the backing. Cut the batting, and baste the layers together.

❖ **Finishing:** Quilt as marked or as desired. Make a binding from the light fabric and attach it all around.

An 1859 cottonwood cabin with whitewashed walls gives a fitting picture of what life was like in the mid-1800s in Nebraska's Platte River Valley (right). Then, this room would have served as both bedroom and living room. The One-Patch quilt in the cradle and the Turkey Tracks quilt on the bed represent the kind of handwork typically done by pioneer women, who often worked in the evenings by firelight - after a day of hard labor. Much of the quilting was done during the winter, when the farm's always-substantial workload subsided a bit. This cabin is part of the Stuhr Museum of the Prairie Pioneer in Grand Island, Nebraska.

Ohio Star Quilt

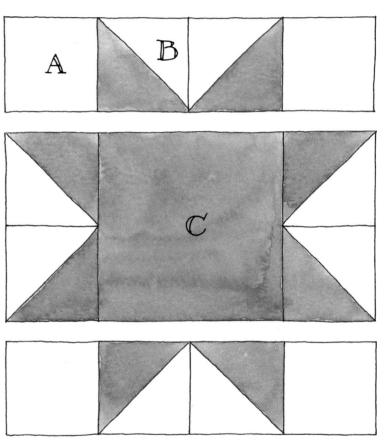

QUILT BLOCK ASSEMBLY

DIRECTIONS

❖ **Notes:** The fabrics used for the patches on the quilt shown here vary from block to block, but all of them retain the same amount of contrast of dark for the star and light for the background. For simplicity, these directions refer to light- and dark-colored fabric.

Read the Quiltmaking Basics and refer to them throughout. Remember that seam allowances must be added when cutting all pieces.

❖ **Preparing Templates:** Make templates as follows: For patches, A is a 2" (5.1 cm) square, B is the triangle that results from cutting a 2" square diagonally in half, and C is a 4" (10.2 cm) square. Also make a template for a plain 8" (20.3 cm) square.

❖ **Cutting Patches and Plain Blocks:** For each Ohio Star block (make 50), cut 4 A and 8 B from light fabric and 1 C and 8 B from dark fabric. Use the plain square template to cut 50 blocks from another fabric.

❖ Making Each Block: Make 50 blocks in all. Join the B patches together in unmatched pairs along their long edges to form square units. Stitch the square units together in pairs with the light fabric sides together, forming a rectangle with a large light-colored triangle in the center. Arrange the patches and units as shown in the Assembly Diagram. Stitch the patches and units together into horizontal rows, then stitch the rows together, taking care to match seams.

❖ Assembling the Quilt Top: Alternate Ohio Star blocks and plain blocks in a checkerboard pattern of 10 rows of 10. If assorted fabrics are used, play around with the positions of the star blocks until the arrangement is satisfying. Stitch the blocks together in horizontal rows, then stitch the rows together, taking care to match the seams.

❖ Making the Backing and Borders: Cut the backing first from 3 strips of cloth 90" (228.6 cm) long. Stitch these together along the selvages. Trim from both sides to obtain a 90" square. Using the fabric trimmed away, cut 4 border strips 4" x 90" (10.2 x 228.6 cm). Stitch a strip to each side of the quilt top, mitering the corners.

❖ Assembling the Quilt: Mark the quilt top for quilting, if desired. Piece the backing, cut the batting, and baste the layers together.

❖ Finishing: Quilt as marked or as desired. As shown, the quilt features standard quilting along the darker patches making up the Ohio Star and parallel diagonal lines along the plain blocks, extending into the lighter patches that form the background of the star.

Use the fabric left over after cutting out the plain blocks to make a binding and attach it all around.

Time has stolen the earliest examples of quilting. Old fibers have simply worn away. This much is known about the origins of quilting: Piecing fabrics is an ancient art. Egyptians were sewing checkerboard designs thousands of years before Christ was born. The history of wearing quilted clothing goes back centuries in China. Quilted mats and coverlets were used by the Romans, while embroidered quilts were made in ancient India. Quilted clothing and banners were common in medieval times. Knights wore quilted long johns under their shining armor. And when trade began with the Far East, pieced Chinese silks and brocades made their way to an eager European audience.

A Sicilian linen quilt, made with flat quilting and trapunto work around 1400, is in the Victoria and Albert Museum in London. The oldest surviving pieced English quilt, dated 1708, is made from pieces of Indian chintz fabrics and quilted with bright red thread instead of the traditional white. (Even then, quilters were expressing individuality through their handwork.) The oldest surviving American quilt was made around 1780.

An Irish Chain quilt tops a nineteenth-century French bed (opposite). Pieces originally cut for a Log Cabin quilt have been sewn into a striking pillow. The bed's bottom and headboard are upholstered with homespun linen sheets, and beneath the mattress a *bedboard, wrapped in foam, is covered with yet another pieced quilt. A wall-mounted shelf, lit from below, makes a handy bedside table.*

Quilting as a way of decorating clothing and bedcovers was popular throughout Europe during the seventeenth and eighteenth centuries. Most likely, the craft of quiltmaking came across the ocean with the first English settlers. In the New World, American quilters gave their own spin to the craft. Quilted garments eventually lost favor, but quiltmaking reached greater artistic and technical heights than it ever had in Europe. Even today, the quilting fever embracing so many modern American women is just starting to infect the Europeans.

In the eighteenth and nineteenth centuries, youngsters were taught to sew as part of a proper education. Mother demonstrated the proper way to stitch, her tiny, even stitches contrasting sharply with her child's first efforts. Young fingers, just becoming coordinated, fumbled with the sharp needle and finicky thread until, finally, they could control the two. After that, magic! Real sewing could begin.

Along with their instruction in all the various embroidery stitches, children were taught to piece. Their first attempts included joining small squares of fabric to create a design called the One-Patch, and from there they graduated to Four-Patch and Nine-Patch designs, until they were proficient enough to make an actual quilt top.

Boys quilted, too. At age 10, Calvin Coolidge cut the pieces for a Baby Blocks quilt that is now on display at his homestead in Plymouth Notch, Vermont. Dwight Eisenhower and his brothers helped their mother make a Tumbling Blocks quilt from shirt and dress scraps. It can be seen at the president's birthplace museum in Denison, Texas.

A Victorian brass tester bed is simply dressed (above) with a Double Irish Chain quilt probably made during the early twentieth century, when this pattern was very popular for everyday quilts. A folded Bow Ties quilt lies at the foot of the bed. A woodsy-toned Nine-Patch covers a new twig bed (right). The Friendship Album quilt on top has a signature in every block. (Directions for making the Friendship Album quilt are on pages 54–55.) More quilts are displayed in the blue cupboard, its open door revealing a Postage Stamp quilt. A bedroom dazzles the eye with an array of wonderful objects (opposite). A whole-cloth quilt of vintage fabric is folded at the foot of the bed, and a Radiant Stars quilt is slung over the footrail. The bedside table includes a Crazy Quilt dripping with fringe.

Friendship Album Quilt

DIRECTIONS

❖ **Notes:** This quilt is traditionally a group project, with one person making each block and signing her name across the rectangular center patch. If this is being done by a group, the group may decide to tailor the number of blocks or revise the Assembly Diagram to its own specifications. As shown, the quilt uses one fabric consistently for the light patches and sashing, while the darker fabric varies from block to block. For simplicity, the directions refer to light- and dark-colored fabric.

Read the Quiltmaking Basics and refer to them throughout. Remember that seam allowances must be added when cutting all pieces.

❖ **Preparing Templates:** Make templates for patches as follows: A is a rectangle 1 ¼" x 3 ¾" (3.2 x 9.5 cm) and B is a 1 ¼" (3.2 cm) square. Also make a template for a half block C, which is the triangle formed by cutting a 7" (17.8 cm) square diagonally in half, and make another for a short sashing strip D, which is 1 ¾" x 7" (4.5 x 17.8 cm).

❖ **Cutting Patches:** For each friendship block (this quilt contains 60), cut out 1 A and 18 B from the light fabric and 4 A and 8 B from the dark fabric.

❖ **Autographing the Quilt:** Sign a name (and any other significant data) across the center of each light A patch with embroidery stitches or a fabric pen. If working with a pen, press with a dry iron, using a press-cloth to heat-set the ink.

❖ **Making Each Block:** Begin with a center unit: Arrange patches as shown in Figure 1. Stitch the Bs together for the top and bottom horizontal rows, then stitch the rows together. Follow Figure 2 and arrange 1 dark A and B and 3 light B patches to form 4 units. On 2 of the units, add 2 light B patches to complete a pyramid shape. Stitch the patches in rows, then stitch the rows together, taking care to match the seams. Join these units around the center unit as

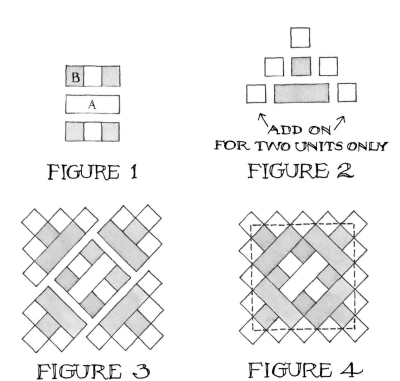

B A

FIGURE 1

ADD ON
FOR TWO UNITS ONLY

FIGURE 2

FIGURE 3

FIGURE 4

ASSEMBLY DIAGRAM

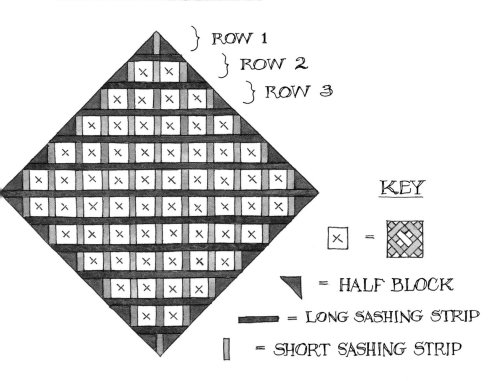

} ROW 1
} ROW 2
} ROW 3

KEY

⊠ = (block design)

◣ = HALF BLOCK

▬ = LONG SASHING STRIP

▮ = SHORT SASHING STRIP

shown in Figure 3; stitch the smaller units to either side of the center unit; then stitch the larger units at the top and bottom, matching the seams. Mark a line connecting the outer corners of the dark fabric patches, as shown in Figure 4; trim away a seam allowance's width beyond the marked line.

❖ **Making Half Blocks:** Use template C to cut 24 half blocks from Fabric 1.

❖ **Cutting Sashing:** Mark and cut Fabric 2 lengthwise into 10 strips 1 ¾" (4.5 cm) wide. Use template D to cut 72 short sashing strips from some of these strips.

❖ **Assembling the Quilt Top:** Referring to the Assembly Diagram, arrange the friendship blocks on point, with the short sashing strips on either side. Place long sashing strips between the rows, cutting from the 1 ¾"-wide strips as needed. Add half blocks all around. Stitch pieces together in horizontal rows, as shown; then stitch the rows together, taking care to align the blocks and short sashing strips.

❖ **Assembling the Quilt:** Mark the quilt top for quilting. The quilt shown has a simple chain link design along the sashing strips. Piece the backing, cut the batting, and baste the layers together.

❖ **Finishing:** Quilt as marked or as desired. On the quilt shown, each patch of the block is quilted ¼" (0.6 cm) from each edge (in addition to the chain link design). Make a binding from Fabric 2 and attach it all around.

Before visitors arrive in the guest room, with its Mariner's Compass quilt from Indiana and the Irish Chain quilt from Arkansas (left), they must pass through a blue hallway in this guest cottage, newly built from old wood. There, a small hooked rug and framed floral appliqué quilt block with a sawtooth border reveal the owner's fondness for the textiles she has found on antiquing jaunts throughout America. The quilt block was hung to honor the anonymous quilter who attempted this difficult pattern in miniature. A homemade Four-Patch-Squares quilt, a nineteenth-century cannonball bed, and a glowing hearth are a winning combination in this guest room under the eaves (opposite top). (Directions for making the Four-Patch Squares quilt are on pages 58-59.) Pine paneling from the living room was installed here to add more warmth to the surroundings. Laid against a simple gray blanket, an Amish quilt in a variation of the Irish Chain pattern has a chance to show its graphic punch (opposite below). Curtains stitched from dishtowels are tied to the curtain rod. The blue bed ruffle and red turkeywork pillow sham provide bright accents to a boy's room in a 1780s house in Maine.

Even among adults, quilting has never been solely a female pursuit. An old painting depicts a Civil War soldier, recuperating in bed, making a quilt. Though rare, a few of the twentieth century's most innovative quilts have been made by men.

A room can take on a masculine look or project a manly feeling depending on the quilt that lives there. The color, the strength of that color, and the overall design can contribute to that look. For example, instead of an open, airy appliqué quilt, a denser pieced quilt of stripes, stars, checks, or repeating boxes may be perfect for a young boy's or a man's room. Geometric patterns provide a masculine tone, as do Amish quilts, which make dramatic use of large blocks of solid color and bold, simpler designs. (For more on Amish quilts, see page 98.)

Four-Patch Squares Quilt

THE ESSENTIALS

FINISHED SIZE

86" (218.4 cm) square

MATERIALS

5 yards (4.6 m) for backing

•

For patches, ½ yard (45.7 cm) each from 4 different fabrics (Fabrics 1, 2, 3, and 4) or scraps from assorted fabrics (see the section on "Cutting Patches"), 1 ⅜ yard (1.3 m) of a fifth fabric (Fabric 5), 2 ½ yards (2.3 m) for sashing and borders (may be the same as Fabrics 1, 2, 3, or 4, or a different, sixth fabric)

Sewing thread in ecru and colors to match Fabric 5, sashing, and borders

•

Batting

Additional supplies as listed in the Quiltmaking Basics on page 185

DIRECTIONS

❖ **Note:** Read over the Quiltmaking Basics and refer to them throughout. Remember that seam allowances must be added to all dimensions or when cutting all patches.

❖ **Preparing Templates:** Make templates: A is a 1 ¾" (4.5 cm) square, and B is the triangle formed when a 5" (12.7 cm) square is cut diagonally in half.

❖ **Cutting Patches:** In the quilt shown, the same fabric is used for Fabrics 1, 2, 3, and 4 within each block, but changes from block to block. Either follow this plan, or keep all the blocks consistent.

For each block (make 25), cut 4 A each from Fabrics 1, 2, 3, and 4 and 4 B from Fabric 5.

❖ **Making Each Block:** Arrange 2 units of 4-patch following the diagram for Unit I and 2 following the diagram for Unit II. Stitch the patches together in each unit: First, join the horizontal pairs, then stitch the pairs together, taking care to match the center seams. Next, arrange the 4 units of Four-Patch together as shown in the diagram for the Inner Block, and stitch the pieces together in the same manner as for the units. Finally, stitch a B patch to each side of the Inner Block; see the diagram for the Complete Quilt Block, which should measure 10" (25.4 cm) square within seam allowances.

❖ **Cutting Borders and Sashing:** First, cut the borders: 4 strips 4" x 88" (10.2 x 223.5 cm). Next, cut the sashing strips: 4 strips 2" x 60" (5.1 x 152.4 cm) and 20 short strips 2" x 10" (5.1 x 25.4 cm).

❖ **Assembling the Quilt Top:** Arrange quilt blocks in 5 rows of 5, moving

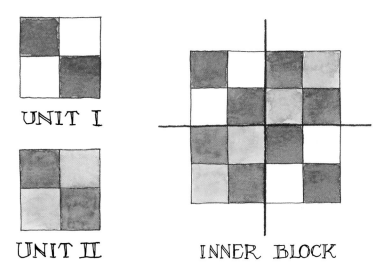

UNIT I

UNIT II

INNER BLOCK

COMPLETE QUILT BLOCK

FABRIC KEY

■ = FABRIC 1

□ = FABRIC 2

■ = FABRIC 3

■ = FABRIC 4

■ = FABRIC 5

blocks around until they look pleasing. Place a long sashing strip between the vertical rows and a short sashing strip between the squares within each vertical row. Stitch the vertical rows together, joining the sashing strips to the squares. Trim the long sashing strips to match, then stitch the vertical rows together. Stitch a border strip to the top and bottom of the quilt top. Trim the ends even with the quilt top, then stitch the remaining strips to the sides of the quilt top.

❖ **Assembling the Quilt:** Mark the quilt top for quilting if desired. Piece the backing, cut the batting, and baste the layers together.

❖ **Finishing:** Quilt as marked or as desired. For simple geometric quilting, use tape as a guide for stitches. As shown, the quilting for each inner block divides each patch diagonally in half in both directions, and B patches are quilted with 2 smaller concentric triangles [use ¾"-wide (1.9 cm) tape]. Sashes are quilted in parallel lines along lengthwise centers, and borders are quilted in parallel lines 1" (2.5 cm) apart on the diagonal.

Make a binding and attach it all around the quilt.

The star is one of the most popular motifs in the history of American quilting. Over one hundred variations of the basic Star pattern have been documented. Difficult to sew because of their many intricate pieces, Star quilts were often saved strictly for company. They are shown to best advantage spread out on a bed or displayed on a wall, where the design can be appreciated in its entirety.

The Star is a patchwork pattern made up of a combination of squares, diamonds, and triangles. The maker of such a quilt must have a highly developed sense of color because the pattern radiates from the center and, when properly executed, can appear to pulsate.

The Star of Bethlehem is a basic, classic pattern. It has eight large points, each consisting of 48 equal-size diamonds. Beautiful examples were made by the Mennonite community during the late nineteenth century. The Lone Star, a favorite among the Amish in Lancaster County, Pennsylvania, is a variation often made with a dark background to set off the star's brilliance. The Feathered, or Sawtooth, Star is a square surrounded by a pattern of small triangles. Some Star variations may have one large star or a pattern of several small ones. The Broken Star is an example of a central star surrounded by separate points radiating into the background; it is one of the most dramatic of all the pattern's variations. Typical borders for the star often incorporate appliqué vine and floral patterns.

A new Radiant Star quilt from Amish quilters commands center stage in this bedroom (right), its only visual challenge the 1820 Pennsylvania German cupboard decorated with a dozen different kinds of graining. (Directions for making the Radiant Star quilt are on pages 62–63.) Bedrooms tend to be chilly in an eighteenth-century stone house in Pennsylvania (opposite), so the owners use quilts to stay warm while enjoying their visual warmth at the same time. The brilliant colors of this Star of Bethlehem quilt stand out against woodwork painted James Getty tan, a Williamsburg color. The rope bed, circa 1840, has a blanket rail for hanging extra covers in winter.

Radiant Star Quilt

DIRECTIONS

❖ **Notes:** Read over the Quiltmaking Basics and refer to them throughout. While it is not necessary to work with a template using the alternate strip piecing method, seam allowances will be needed when cutting all strips and all pieces.

❖ **Working in Traditional Patchwork:** Use the actual-size pattern on page 193

to make a diamond template. Use the template to cut 80 diamonds from Fabric 1, 64 each from Fabrics 2, 3, 4, 5, and 6, and 56 each from Fabrics 7 and 8. Following Figure 3, arrange the small diamonds into a large diamond for each star point. Sew the diamonds together to make each row (A through H); then sew the rows together, taking care to match the seams.

❖ **Working in the Alternate Strip Piecing Method:** Mark and cut lines across the entire width of Fabrics 1 through 8 to make strips 1 ⅜" (3.5 cm) wide plus seam allowances; ¼" (0.6 cm) seam allowance is recommended for diamonds, so the total width of the strips should be 1 ⅞" (4.8 cm). Make 16 strips from Fabric 1, 8 strips each from Fabrics 2 through 8. Take one strip each from Fabrics 1 through 7 and place them side by side; then repeat a Fabric 1 strip on the opposite edge. To save fabric, stagger the strips by 1" (2.5 cm) (see Figure 2), then stitch them together. Press the seams to one side, with the exception of

Take some time to plan a palette. Photocopy the star diagram (Figure 1) several times, and experiment with various color arrangements. Use markers or colored pencils to fill in the color key and the correspondingly numbered diamond shapes. For a star that appears to radiate, select colors in the order they appear in the color spectrum. Another possibility is to use 1, 2, or 3 colors broken down into shades that gradually move from light to dark or from pale to bright. After establishing a palette, select fabrics to correspond with the key. It may help to cut out patches from the actual fabric and glue them on an enlarged version of the star diagram. This kind of planning ensures that one will be happy with the chosen fabrics and arrangement before actually cutting and sewing. A good way to select the best background (Fabric 9) is to actually cut out the mosaic star and lay it on top of various fabrics.

FIGURE 1. STAR DIAGRAM

very light fabrics, which should be pressed toward the darker fabric.

Using the triangle, mark across the strips at a 45° angle, close to the staggered end. Make a template strip exactly 1 ⅜" plus seam allowances, or 1 ⅞" wide, and 23" (58.4 cm) long. Use this template to mark lines that are a template's width apart across the fabric, simultaneously using the triangle to double check for 45° angles. Make 8 strips along the diagonal in this fashion. Place these strips in a baggie or neat pile and label "A." In the same way, refer to Figure 3 to make 8 strips in the sequences shown for rows B, C, D, E, F, G, and H.

For each star point, take a strip from each pile and lay out the strips as shown in Figure 3. Pin the strips together, inserting a pin at the seam line through each of the points of the diamond patches of both strips. Stitch, removing each pin just before machine-stitching over the corresponding diamond point.

Make all 8 star points exactly the same; they should all measure 15" (38.1 cm) along each side, within the seam allowances.

❖ **Assembling the Star:** Arrange all 8 points as shown in Figure 1, so that Fabric 2 is placed 1 patch away from the center. Sew points together as shown in Figure 4; begin and end the stitching at the diamond point on the seam line, so that the stitching does not extend into the seam allowances on the first and last patch. Pin generously, taking care to

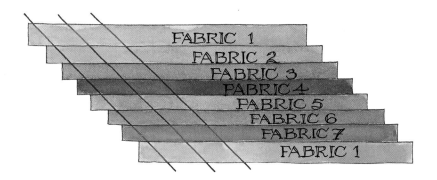

FIGURE 2. COMBINATION STRIP A

COMBINATION STRIPS

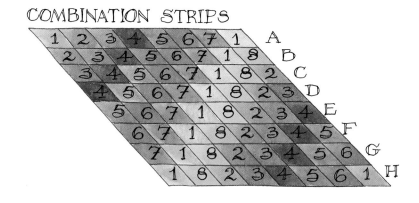

FIGURE 3. STAR POINT

FABRIC KEY

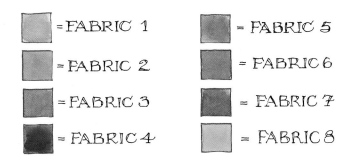

= FABRIC 1   = FABRIC 5

= FABRIC 2   = FABRIC 6

= FABRIC 3   = FABRIC 7

= FABRIC 4   = FABRIC 8

It takes hours of work to make an intricate floral appliqué quilt like the one covering the high tester bed of a grand and spacious bedroom (left). A warm Plume appliqué quilt with a swag border tops a four-poster (above). (Directions for making the Plume quilt are on pages 72–73.) The top was made in the mid-1800s in Ohio but was never sewn into a quilt until its present owner found old batting and muslin and asked a local quilting shop to sandwich all the layers together.

Rightly or wrongly, appliqué quilts have always been more highly valued than their patchwork cousins. Chintz quilts were the earliest form of appliqué, made by cutting out floral motifs from colorful imported Indian chintzes and sewing them to a solid ground. Quilts employing this technique are termed *borderie perse* and were made between 1790 and 1850. Such quilts were a thrifty way of stretching a treasured piece of imported fabric or salvaging good parts after the rest of the fabric had worn out.

By the nineteenth century, American quiltmakers had produced many different appliqué patterns. Sometimes, an assortment were combined in an Album quilt. The fanciest of such works were made by women in Baltimore in the 1850s as friendship projects to give to a minister or to a neighbor moving away. They included such intricate designs as wreaths, garlands, and bouquets. In her book, *Spoken Without a Word*, Elly Sienkiewicz surmises that the shapes were symbolic: For example, acanthus leaves expressed admiration for the fine arts, a book represented the Bible, and oak leaves stood for courage. These quilts gave women a chance to show how fine their handwork was.

Plume Quilt

DIRECTIONS

❖ **Notes:** To avoid the bulk of multiple appliqué layers, reverse appliqué is occasionally used in this quilt. That means, instead of overlapping shapes, fabric is cut away to reveal an underlayer.

Read the Quiltmaking Basics and refer to them throughout. Remember that seam allowances must be added when cutting all pieces.

❖ **Preparing Templates:** Trace the actual-size patterns for pieces A through I shown on pages 193-195, and make templates. Template A is a solid piece, but B has a ½" (1.3 cm) hole, or opening, cut out of the center and C has an oval opening cut out of its center. Template D is 1 piece that is overlapped by a centered E strip. Make separate templates for H and I.

❖ **Cutting the Background:** For the background of the quilt top, mark and cut the following pieces, leaving ½" seam allowances: 4 squares 34" (86.4 cm) and 4 border strips 10" x 92" (25.4 x 233.7 cm).

THE ESSENTIALS

FINISHED SIZE

88" (223.5 cm) square

MATERIALS

7 ¼ yards (6.6 m) for backing

•

6 ½ yards (5.9 m) for the background, 2 yards (1.8 m) each of Fabric 1 (here, red) and Fabric 3 (here, dark teal), and 1 ¼ yards (1.1 m) of Fabric 2 (here, yellow) for appliqués

•

Sewing thread to match the fabrics

•

Batting

•

Additional supplies as listed in the Quiltmaking Basics on page 185

❖ **Preparing Appliqués:** On each B and C piece, cut out just ⅛" (0.3 cm) to the inside of the marked opening. From Fabric 1, cut 61 A, 14 E, and 24 F. From Fabric 2, cut 61 B, 14 D, and 24 G. From Fabric 3, cut 14 C, 24 H, and 24 I.

For each star, baste a B on the center of an A. For each leaf, press the long edges under on an E appliqué and center over a D. Baste both under the opening on a C appliqué piece. For each plume, baste a G over the outside curve

of an F, and baste an H over the outside curve of the same G. Baste each swag in the same way, but use an I appliqué instead of the H.

❖ **Sewing Appliqués:** Refer to the Appliqué Diagram, which shows one-quarter of the quilt top. Position each piece and pin it to the background. Adjust the spacing as indicated or as desired. Baste the appliqués to the background, turning the seam allowance of each overlapping edge to the wrong side. Use matching thread to slip-stitch each piece in place.

For each block, pin a star at the exact center of each background square. Place the plumes around the star, spacing them evenly, with one point at each star tip. The plumes should radiate out from the center and all curve in the same direction. At the opposite end of each plume, pin a star. Appliqué all the pieces in place.

❖ **Assembling the Quilt Top:** Working ½" (1.3 cm) from the edges, stitch the 4 squares together to form 1 large square.

APPLIQUÉ DIAGRAM:
ONE QUARTER OF QUILT TOP

Over the center where the 4 squares join, appliqué 1 star and 4 leaves, 1 over each seam.

❖ **Adding the Border:** Center the border strips along each side of the quilt top. Stitch them in place, sewing ½" from the edges and staying inside the seam allowances at the ends. Miter the ends of the border strips at each corner. Pin appliqué pieces close to the seam along the border strips as follows: Place a star at the midpoint of each side and at each corner. Position 2 stars, evenly spaced, between these stars. Pin swags between the stars. Appliqué these pieces in place. Add the remaining leaf shapes as suggested on the quilt diagram. Turning the leaves on a slight angle will result in a lighter, more organic effect.

❖ **Assembling the Quilt:** Mark the quilt top for quilting as desired. On the quilt shown, each H piece features lines of echo quilting about ½" (1.3 cm) apart. Note that the echo quilting follows the contours of each spinning set of plumes and stars. A scroll design follows the swag and star border and embellishes the background fabric edges beyond the border. Piece the backing, cut the batting, and baste the layers together.

❖ **Finishing:** Quilt as marked or as desired. Make a binding from Fabric 1 and attach it all around.

Crazy quilts are the gypsies of the quilt world. Forget 100 percent cotton ~ the Crazy quilt flaunts its fancy silk, satin, and velvet patches, its extravagant embroidery, its ribbon, bead, and sequin embellishments. Words and even messages have been known to be ensconced in a Crazy quilt's construction.

A Crazy quilt ~ its name implies a haphazard state ~ is a form of patchwork in which overlapping fabric pieces are randomly arranged on a base fabric. Though folklore has it that Crazy quilts evolved from humble origins ~ well-worn quilts mended with patches that didn't match ~ current research indicates that is not the case. Crazy quilts became enormously popular status symbols during the Victorian era among wealthy women, who could shown off their affluence by lavishing them with fancy materials and rich decorations.

The Crazy quilt is made for great gestures. Flung across a piano, draped on a curvy chaise in the parlor, or mounted on the wall, it is in its element. Often a Crazy quilt, with its bright colors and sensuous fabrics, can give a country-style room just the right sparkle.

A 1928 Ohio Album scrap quilt (above) combines patchwork, appliqué, and embroidery techniques. An old red shirt and calico apron were cut up for the many different posies. The contained Crazy quilt on the wall (opposite) and an appliqué wool coverlet on the bed both use black with dramatic results. The effect is

heightened by the thick, brightly colored stitches running throughout both pieces. The Crazy quilt's embroidered velvet patches were probably saved from special dresses the maker did not want to part with. (Directions for making a Crazy quilt are on page 94.)

Growing up with Quilts

Miniature quilts have traditionally been used as coverings for a baby's cradle or crib. Some of these were simply scaled-down versions of contemporary patterns, made to match other family bed-coverings. Other quiltmakers developed new motifs specifically for cribs.

The names of crib quilts provide a clue to their designs: Baby Blocks, Building Blocks, Sunbonnet Sue, and Tumbling Blocks are just a few. In Victorian times, a central pictorial panel surrounded by squares or patches was a favorite style. Pastel quilts, popular from 1920 to 1940, are also perfect for a young child's room. Dresden Plates, Butterflies, Sunburst designs ~ any work with graphic simplicity and softness provides a bright, fresh look. Grandmother's Flower Garden is a popular pattern for children's rooms because of its gaiety and color. Hexagonal pieces of fabric are arranged in concentric circles to resemble flowers, each surrounded by a grid of contrasting fabric. This arrangement is a variation of the One-Patch, where the overall design is made by joining patches together one by

one. Many such quilts were made during the Depression because very small scraps could be used.

Today's popular patterns for crib quilts include all the old favorites, as well as new designs incorporating such motifs as animals, sailboats, houses, and toys, rendered in bright, cheerful colors. Scenic and pictorial appliqué quilts are especially appropriate for the nursery. Rhymes and songs can be embroidered, and buttons and bows added. Appliqué hearts, birds, flowers, and animals appeal to the child in everyone.

In the last decade, early-childhood experts have discovered that very young infants can distinguish between black and white more easily than between individual colors. What better way to stimulate an infant's visual senses from birth than with a quilt? In her 1897 book, *The Decoration of Houses*, American author and society matron Edith Wharton declared a child's room incomplete without an "edifying engraving" on the wall. A quilt makes an effective substitute that would surely meet such high standards.

Those who appreciate antique needlework will enjoy hanging framed samples of a child's early pieced work in a youngster's room. During the nineteenth century, girls were versed in the arts of embroidery, sewing, and knitting at a very young age. This was painstaking, laborious work for uncoordinated fingers, so their creations were all the more treasured because of the time and effort that went into making them. Instructions began at home and, for the wealthy, continued at a "dame school," a neighborhood

This little-girl room filled with handmade touches has great appeal (opposite). An early twentieth-century Fan quilt graces the bed, where a home-made rag doll nestles. Other handwork includes a lace-edged table topper and a fringed, old-fashioned rag rug underfoot. The pillows, bedskirt, and valances were newly made from crisp linen dishtowels in a variety of checks, plaids, and stripes. Bouffant balloon shades provide frothy contrast.

kindergarten that little boys also attended. Some of the youngsters' earliest attempts have survived in the form of long, narrow samplers and simple piecework.

It is important when shopping for an antique crib quilt to verify that the work is the real thing. Some crib quilts may actually be pieces of damaged full-size counterpanes that have been cut down by unscrupulous dealers seeking to pass them off as originals. Of course, thrifty pioneers may have recycled their worn-out bedcoverings this way. The binding, stitches, and type of thread are all clues when evaluating the authenticity of a crib coverlet.

Crib quilts also make popular wallhangings because of their small size. One proud aunt created a lasting gift for a newborn nephew by sending a white cotton quilt block to each of her relatives. They were instructed to draw a picture on the block with indelible heat-set crayons; the funniest turned out to be a cartoon duck quacking "Don't sass your mother." After all the blocks were returned to her, she stitched the quilt together by interspersing the blocks with pastel gingham blocks and highlighting certain features of each block with embroidery. The quilt was used as a blanket when the child was young; now it hangs in his bedroom, a treasured memento of his birth.

An imaginative way to use baby clothes a child has outgrown is to make a quilt from patches cut from them. Or a family quilt can be assembled from cast-off clothing belonging to all members of the family.

The enterprising sewer might fashion a quilted sleeping bag for a youngster who likes sleepovers at home or away. And what child would want to travel without a "quillow," a light, soft quilt that becomes a pillow when folded into thirds, rolled up, and tucked into a pocket sewn to the center back of the quilt.

Many children's rooms contain a rocking chair. This is the place to put a pillow made from quilt scraps or unused pieced blocks. Even someone who has never quilted before or knows she will not have the patience to complete an entire quilt can start small with a handmade pillow.

A Grandmother's Flower Garden quilt looks delightful in a girl's room populated by Raggedy Anns of all ages (above). The bold Mill Wheel crib quilt on the wall of a baby's room (opposite) keeps one's eye entertained for hours with its ever-changing optical pattern. (Directions for making the Mill Wheel crib quilt are on pages 80–81.)

Mill Wheel Crib Quilt

┌─────────────────────────────────┐
│ **THE ESSENTIALS**

FINISHED SIZE

25" x 30" (63.5 x 76.2 cm)

MATERIALS

¾ yard (68.6 cm) for backing

•

⅝ yard (57.2 cm) each of light- and dark-colored fabrics for patches, ½ yard (45.7 cm) for binding (the same dark fabric was used here)

•

White sewing thread

•

Batting

•

Additional supplies as listed in the Quiltmaking Basics on page 185
└─────────────────────────────────┘

DIRECTIONS

❖ **Notes:** This quilt is a variation of a Rob-Peter-to-Pay-Paul pattern, so-called because the way the wedges are cut out of the corners of each block makes it seem that a light patch has "robbed" a dark patch of space, and vice versa.

Read the Quiltmaking Basics and refer to them throughout. Remember that seam allowances must be added when cutting all pieces.

❖ **Preparing Templates:** Trace the actual-size patterns for A and B on page 196 and use these to make templates.

❖ **Cutting Patches:** When cutting, place as many straight edges as possible along the grain of the fabric. Cut 30 A and 60 B from both light and dark fabrics.

❖ **Making Each Block:** Join 2 light B patches to each dark A to form a triangle. To join curved edges, place pieces together with right sides facing, and pin through both pieces on the marked line. First, pin at both ends of the curve, then pin at the midpoints, then slightly stretch the inner curve of the A patch to match the curve of the B patch and add other pins in between. Hand-stitch or hand-baste along the marked line, extending the stitching line into the seam allowances so that stitching begins and ends at the fabric edges. Ease the curved edge of the A patch while working. Remove the pins. For machine-piecing, follow the hand-basted stitches, easing the fabric while sewing. Press the seam allowances toward the darker patch.

In the same manner, make another triangle with the colors reversed. To complete the block, stitch the 2 triangles together along the long edges, taking care to match the seams. The result is a 5" (12.7 cm) square within the seam allowances. Repeat this technique to make a total of 30 blocks.

❖ **Assembling the Quilt Top:** Arrange the blocks in 6 rows of 5. Refer to the numbers along the sides of the Quilt Block Diagram; they indicate which side should be at the top for each position. For example, when the number 1 is at the top, there is a dark wedge at the upper-left corner. Following the assembly diagram, rotate each block so that the number of each corresponding square correctly indicates which side of the block is at the top. Adjacent blocks should form circles with wedges of alternating colors. Stitch the blocks together in horizontal rows, taking care to match the seams. Then carefully stitch the rows together.

❖ **Assembling the Quilt:** Mark the quilt top for quilting, if desired. Cut the backing and the batting, and baste the layers together.

❖ **Finishing:** Quilt in or near the seams of the patches or perhaps around the circular units. Use the dark fabric to make a binding and attach it all around.

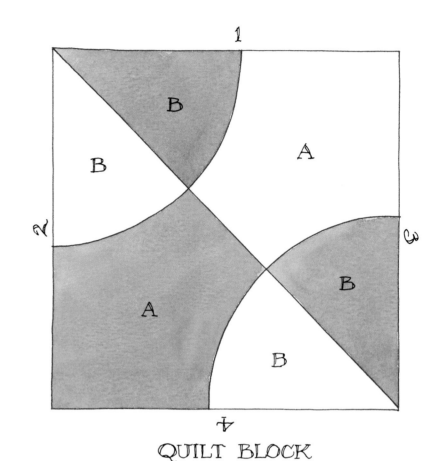

QUILT BLOCK

1	2	1	2	1
3	4	3	4	3
1	2	1	2	1
3	4	3	4	3
1	2	1	2	1
3	4	3	4	3

ASSEMBLY DIAGRAM

Below a four-poster, a trundle bed made from a kit is covered with a Double Wedding Ring quilt (left). It comes in handy for a sleepover or an unexpected overnight guest. In this guest room in Ohio (opposite), attention is focused on a Dolls quilt, made from a kit, which graces the head of the four-poster rope bed. The bed's plaid throw from New Hampshire and the trundle's old feather tick wrapped in new stripes are other inviting features. The bed and trundle are reproductions that were crafted by a furniture maker.

Miniature House Quilt

THE ESSENTIALS

FINISHED SIZE

11 ½" (29.2 cm) square

•

MATERIALS

18" (45.7 cm) for backing, borders, and sashing strips

•

4 ½" (11.4 cm) each of 3 prints (for house, roof, and background) and one solid (for chimneys and house edging), plus scraps of assorted prints (for doors and windows; see Notes)

•

Sewing thread to match fabrics

•

Batting

•

A clear, thick sheet of plastic such as acetate (sold in art supply stores)

•

Ruler

•

A fine, permanent-ink, felt-tip marker

•

Additional supplies as listed in the Quiltmaking Basics on page 185

DIRECTIONS

❖ **Notes:** The maker of this miniature or doll quilt ingeniously chose a gingham [with ¼" (0.6 cm) squares] for the windows, cutting her appliqué piece so that a cross of woven threads would serve to divide the window into panes. For the door, she found a fabric with a widely spaced small motif and positioned her appliqué so the small motif created a doorknob. Choose fabrics with an eye to these special effects. Use the same fabrics for each house, as shown, or vary the fabrics from house to house.

This quilt is finished by turning the backing over on to the quilt top to provide a self-binding border. The directions assume ¼" seam allowances; if otherwise, adjust the measurements in "Assembling the Quilt" so there is a ⅝" (1.6 cm) border all around.

Read over the Quiltmaking Basics and refer to them throughout. Remember that seam allowances must be added when cutting all pieces.

❖ **Preparing Templates:** Instead of making conventional templates, trace or mark the patterns for the house and roof on page 196 on acetate using a ruler and felt-tip marker. (Working with a see-through template allows one to position the shapes easily on the fabric.) Also make a ½" x 1 ¼" (1.3 x 3.2 cm) rectangle and a ¾" (1.9 cm) square for door and window templates, respectively.

❖ **Cutting Pieces:** For each of the 9 quilt blocks, use the templates and mark lightly on the right side of the desired fabrics, positioning the templates appropriately. Cut 1 house, roof, door, and window for each. Also cut a 1" x 3" (2.5 x 7.6 cm) rectangle from a desired fabric for the background (the sky) and a ¼" x 7 ¼" (0.6 x 18.4 cm) strip from solid fabric.

❖ **Making Each Block:** Place the roof so it overlaps the house by ³⁄₁₆" (0.5 cm), and baste along the overlapped edges, as shown in Figure 1. On the long, solid-colored strip, press the seam allowances on the long edges to the wrong side. Adding ¼" (0.6 cm) seam allowances, cut the following lengths: 1 strip 1 ¼" (3.2 cm), 1 strip 3 ¼" (8.2 cm), and 2 strips ½" (1.3 cm). Refer to Figure 2. Without turning under the short ends, pin the 1 ¼" piece across the bottom edge of the roof. Make sure it covers the horizontal, overlapped edge of the roof. Next, pin the 3 ¼" length, beginning from the high point of the roof and covering the sloped, overlapped edge. As it meets and covers the left raw end of the first piece, make it turn a wide angle by taking a little tuck, and continue down on a straight vertical line to the bottom of the block. Appliqué the long edges of these strips. Appliqué the window and door as shown in Figure 2; there is no need to turn under the bottom edge of the door.

Cut the remaining solid strip in half and pin the 2 pieces to the top edge of the background rectangle, as shown in Figure 3. Overlap the background rectangle with the house and adjust the placement of the chimney pieces. Remove the house and appliqué the chimney's side edges. Replace the house on the background, overlapping the background so the entire block measures 3" (7.6 cm) square within the seam allowances (Figure 4). Turn the top edges of the house to the wrong side and slip-stitch inconspicuously along this edge.

❖ **Assembling the Quilt Top:** Cut a 16" (40.6 cm) square for the backing. From

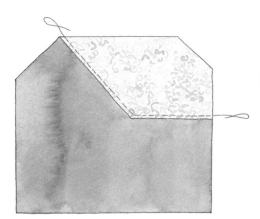

FIGURE 1

FIGURE 2

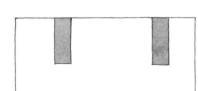

FIGURE 3

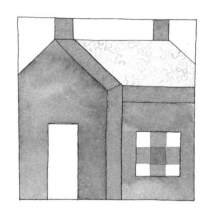

FIGURE 4

the same fabric, make 12 strips ⅝" x 3" (1.6 x 7.6 cm). From the solid fabric, make 4 pieces ⅝" square. Arrange the houses in 3 rows of 3, with a strip between the houses. Place a square at each intersection of strips. Stitch houses and strips, or strips and squares, together within each horizontal row. Stitch the rows together, taking care to match the seams.

❖ **Assembling the Quilt:** Cut the backing ⅞" (2.2 cm) larger than the quilt top all around. Cut the batting ⅜" (1.0 cm) larger than the quilt top all around. Place the backing wrong side up on a work surface, and center the batting on

top. Center the quilt top, right side up, on top of the batting and baste the layers together.

❖ **Finishing:** This quilt has no quilting stitches; however, feel free to quilt or tuft as desired. Press the ¼" (0.6 cm) seam allowance of the backing to the wrong side. Bring the top and bottom edges of the backing over the batting and quilt top, and pin the folded edge to the marked seam allowance lines. Slip-stitch to secure. Finish the side edges in the same way, treating the ends as neatly as possible.

Attics and Quilts ~ Kindred Spirits

In *Little House in the Big Woods*, a classic nineteenth-century tale of a Wisconsin childhood, Laura Ingalls Wilder and her sister Mary snuggled into their loft beds at night, warmed by layers of handmade quilts. A century later a quilted bedcovering is still a necessity on a bed nestled under the eaves. Quilts are as much a part of attic or loft decor as Grandmother's weathered trunk filled with old photographs and forgotten love letters.

Attics and lofts have a special appeal. They epitomize privacy, and because they are located high in the air, they seem to be removed from the troubles of the day. As one decorator remarked, attics and lofts are treehouses for grownups, and quilts are their security blankets.

The architecture of attics and lofts sets off the graphic look of quilts. Exposed beams and high ceilings give such spaces gallerylike simplicity, which helps focus attention on the textiles. Rustic, worn, informal quilts are most suitable here; the simplest, most geometric designs, executed in deep, earthy colors, lend themselves best to these surroundings. Log Cabin, Diamonds and Squares, Bars, Ocean Waves, and Bear's Paw are some appropriate patterns.

The cool, dim environment of a secluded attic or loft seems made for quilts, which fare best away from direct sunlight and heavy traffic. One note of caution: These spaces may not be ideal during the summer months unless they are climate-controlled. A stable environment with 50 percent humidity and a temperature of 60 to 70 degrees is preferred.

Attics and lofts are often spacious enough to accommodate pastimes that require large equipment. Quilting and weaving are ideal here. These remote areas have even been known to promote concentration and inspire creativity by their nostalgic link with the past.

The upstairs bedroom of an early-1800s log house in Ohio is decorated in simple Shaker style (opposite). The pine bed, newly made to look old, is covered with a pieced quilt called an Hourglass or Pinwheel pattern ~ its name depends on how one views it. Since the mattress is queen-size, the full-size quilt is laid sideways on the bed. Homemade curtains were dyed in tea to give them an old-fashioned look. The quilt's colors are echoed in the stenciling that outlines the knee wall behind the bed and the peg rack on the wall.

A patchwork and appliqué quilt, circa 1930, with an unusual ribbon motif, covers a plaid-skirted bed in the loft of a Texas farmhouse (above). The bed is topped with another quilt, a pink-and-white Irish Chain, and blue turkeywork pillow shams. In a historic central Texas homestead (opposite), a Dresden Plate quilt dresses a Texas German bed. Rugged, exposed limestone walls are tamed by treasured quilts and antiques bought in Mexico, Europe, and the United States. The ceiling is painted blue, in keeping with a German custom to have the color of the sky overhead. A child's wagon becomes the perfect bedside table. Running across the crocheted rug is one of the tension rods that helps hold the old building together.

The loft bedroom in this Texas guest house (left) is reminiscent of an upstairs bedroom in a "Sunday house," which German farming families used to keep in town where they could stay overnight during weekly visits to church. Then, as now, quilts and Turkey-red embroidered pillow shams give these lofty spaces a cozy mood. Fresh white curtains made from linen tablecloths brighten the stone walls and wood beams of this room built 130 years ago. The cradle's occupants are warmed by a One-Patch crib quilt.

Crazy Quilt

The traditional Crazy quilt usually incorporates scraps of luxurious fabric such as silk, velvet, satin, and fine wool. The scraps are cut in various angular shapes rather than in consistent shapes as in other forms of patchwork.

DIRECTIONS

❖ **Planning the Quilt:** To make a Crazy quilt, lay out a collection of fabric scraps on a large, flat surface. Cut the pieces wherever and however it is necessary to make them fit together. Place pleasing color combinations adjacent to one another, making sure to space out the same colors so their repetition creates an overall unity. Overlap the pieces about ½" (1.3 cm) and turn under the raw edges of the top piece. If desired, incorporate some wide ribbon in the Crazy quilt; then there is no need to turn under the finished edges. Baste the pieces together.

❖ **Joining the Pieces:** To join the pieces, work over the seams using the decorative embroidery stitches as shown in Embroidery Stitch Details on page 188. Use any of the embroidery stitches; however, light, airy, and expansive stitchery works the best. Combine stitches or add French knots. Double or triple the strands threaded in the needle to make sure the stitchery is optimally effective. Use 1 color to embroider throughout, or use different colors to stitch over each seam.

❖ **Finishing the Quilt:** Trim off the edges of the patches on all sides of the

> ### THE ESSENTIALS
>
> #### FINISHED SIZE
>
> *For a twin-size quilt 69" x 105" (175.3 x 266.7 cm); for a double 84" x 105" (213.4 x 266.7 cm); for a queen 90" x 110" (228.6 x 279.4 cm); and for a king 108" x 110" (274.3 x 279.4 cm)*
>
> #### MATERIALS
>
> *Enough scraps of different materials to make the desired size quilt*
>
> •
>
> *A corresponding amount of lining fabric, such as sateen, for the backing*
>
> •
>
> *Silk, rayon, pearl cotton, or embroidery floss*
>
> •
>
> *Additional supplies as listed in the Quiltmaking Basics on page 185*

quilt top to make straight edges; make sure to square them off. While the quilt shown does not have a border, strips of the same fabric all around the edges would frame the patchwork and thus contain or restrain its craziness. It is not necessary to use a filler or batting with a Crazy quilt, but it does need a backing. Pin the quilt top and the backing that has already been cut together with right sides facing, and stitch all around, leaving an opening for turning along one side. Clip across the seam allowance at the corners and turn the quilt to the right side. Turn the open edges to the inside and slip-stitch them closed. Heavy Crazy quilts should be tied at regular intervals. If desired, add a binding along the edges.

An entry is the perfect place to display stellar quilts. In the hallway of this Connecticut farmhouse (left), an 1820s Mosaic quilt made in Maryland falls bannerlike behind a long deacon's bench graced with needlepoint pillows. This is one of the best places in the house to display a quilt, because it is protected from direct sunlight and there are no strong lights overhead. A colorful kilim runner leads the way to the front entrance, where the single door has been replaced by French doors fitted with antique hardware and glass knobs. In a Colonial-style home in Virginia (opposite), two Feathered Star quilts top an assortment of comforters and homespun linens in an open cupboard. A New England Indian basket crowns the collection.

Quilts ~ Tactile Greetings

Aquilt in an entry sets an immediate tone: People who appreciate art live here. For years, dealers have been spreading the word ~ for the price of a mediocre painting, it is possible to own a great quilt.

An entryway has an important function in any home. Not only does it create a first impression, it serves to welcome the visitor. Making this space hospitable is one of the keys of decorating well. One striking front-hall solution involves hanging a bold quilt on the wall and then accenting it with a slim, graceful table.

Though entrance halls and stairways are usually narrow, they often have wall spaces that are ideal for displaying a quilt. Not only will a quilt make the space look bigger, but it allows a close-up look at intricate stitching, cherished inscriptions, and unusual fabrics. If there are railings, lay quilts over them, either in layers or folded in halves.

It is possible to turn a closet in an entrance hall into a quilt cupboard by removing the door. One couple with an extensive selection of nineteenth- and twentieth-century textiles has a linen closet at the end of a long hallway leading from their front door. Every summer they take the door off the closet and replace the sweaters and sheets inside with their neatly folded collection, so visitors are treated to a colorful display as they walk into the apartment.

Proper lighting can help accent a quilt in an entrance or stairway. Besides illuminating the work, it brings out special stitching or fabric details that might otherwise go unnoticed. If there is a question about what type of lighting to choose, Chapter 3 offers essential advice on the best fixtures for these purposes. If a problem persists, then consult a lighting expert ~ perhaps the person who installed the lighting for the textile exhibits at the local museum.

The Amish, A Quilting Community

Prized for their bold graphic designs, unique color combinations, and fine stitching, Amish quilts are considered a premier American folk art. Quilting became a favored activity of the austere Anabaptist sect after they emigrated to the United States and Canada from Germany and Switzerland over 250 years ago and adapted this craft to their own strict religious standards. While the rest of the country was piecing patterned counterpanes, the earliest known Amish quilts, dating from 1849, 1865, and 1869, are whole-cloth works in solid colors, like the Colonists' earliest linsey-woolsey efforts. Amish bed coverings pieced in patterns did not appear until the 1870s.

Amish quilts always feature solid-colored fabrics; purple, green, blue, and brown are most commonly used. Nineteenth-century quilts from Lancaster County, Pennsylvania, are predominantly earth-colored. Even today each church district decides what colors will be allowed in dress and quilts, though the rules are generally not as specific when it comes to quilting.

Particular fabric and patterns are identified with specific Amish settlements. For instance, pre-1940s quilts from Lancaster County were almost always made of wool, while those sewn in Ohio during the same period were generally made of cotton. Favorite Lancaster County patterns, featuring more subdued colors, include Lone Star, Center Diamond, and Irish Chain. Quilts made in Indiana, Illinois, and Iowa are freer in design and color, even incuding yellow.

Many think that the Amish (often confused with the less conservative Mennonites) introduced the use of black in quilting; their designs incorporating black set up strong, dramatic color contrasts. However, the Amish actually adopted a Victorian trend, making it their own a generation or so later. Though black is rarely found in more conservative Lancaster County quilts, it often appears in those made from the 1920s to the 1940s throughout the Midwestern Amish communities, especially those in Ohio.

The Amish did not cut up their old clothes to make quilts, as is widely believed, though they may have used them to fill in a border or backing if they ran out of fabric. Like most quilters, the Amish got their fabric from door-to-door salesmen, from non-Amish department stores, and by mail order. They did use dressmaking scraps in patterns like Sunshine and Shadows, where bits of fabric are needed.

Often these bedcoverings provide the only decoration, besides calendars, in a simply furnished Amish home. But they also play an important role in community life. Since Amish homes are also their places of worship, specially made quilts are put on the bed three and four times a year, when the church district ~ usually a group of less than thirty people ~ comes to worship. Some of the finest old Amish quilts that survive today, a few

close to one hundred years old, were "Sunday quilts."

Though their religion discourages individual expression, quiltmaking has allowed Amish women to express their creative instincts without giving offense. In fact, the Amish community has always supported activities fostering community and family closeness, so quilting became a vital part of the social life of many women in the Amish community.

Quilts are produced for everyday use or to celebrate the birth of a baby, to raise funds for a church or community cause, or to complete a child's marriage dowry (men sometimes bring quilts to a marriage, too). Since the "English" (the name they use for non-Amish people) discovered Amish work in the late 1960s, quilting has also provided a source of income for these reverent, disciplined folk. Though referred to as the Plain People, the Amish are far from plain if judged by their quilts. Indeed, Amish quilts have become collectors' items all over the globe.

A One-Patch quilt arrayed over a tilt-top table (right) creates a graphic still life inside a new cabin made from old logs. In the upstairs hallway of the Mendon Country Inn in Michigan, quilts are rotated regularly (opposite). Here, Jacob's Ladder and Goose Tracks quilts decorate the walls. A Birds in Flight quilt and an Ocean Waves quilt are folded over the back of a century-old church pew transformed with coats of Colonial blue paint. A Rail Fence pillow and an Ohio Stars pillow cushion either end of the pew. At the far end of the hall, a Pinwheel quilt hangs on a quilt rack.

Flower Basket Quilt

DIRECTIONS

❖ **Notes:** The basket block is a combination of patchwork and appliqué, further embellished with embroidery and lattice sashing. The quilt features baskets turned toward the center in a symmetrical arrangement and an extra border at the top, or "heading."

Read the Quiltmaking Basics and refer to them throughout. Remember that seam allowances must be added when cutting all pieces.

❖ **Preparing Templates:** Make templates for the lattice sashing as follows: a 1 ½" x 9" (3.8 x 22.9 cm) strip and a 4 ½" (11.4 cm) square. Make templates for the basket patches as follows (see page 197 for actual-size patterns): A is the triangle that results when a 1 ½" (3.8 cm) square is cut diagonally in half; for B, trace the trapezoid given; C is the triangle that results when a 3" (7.6 cm) square is cut diagonally in half; for D, trace the quadrangle given; F is the triangle that results when a 9" (22.9 cm) square is cut diagonally in half. Also trace the pattern for E and use it to make a template for the handle appliqué.

❖ **Cutting Heading Strips:** Cut a strip 3" x 88" (7.6 x 223.5 cm) from both light and dark fabrics. Set these aside.

❖ **Cutting the Lattice Sashing:** Use the templates to cut pieces for the lattice sashing. From the light fabric, cut 84 strips. From the dark fabric, cut 168 strips and 49 squares. Set these aside.

❖ **Cutting Patches:** For each of 36 blocks, cut the following from the light fabric: 6 A, 1 C, 2 D (reversing the template for the second of the pair), and 1 F. Cut the following pieces from the same dark fabric, or use a different fabric from block to block: 9 A and 1 B for the patches and 1 E for the handle appliqué.

- ❖ **Making Each Block:** Arrange all the pieces as shown in the Quilt Block Diagram.

- ❖ **Assembling the Patchwork:** Join the patches together within each unit, as indicated by the heavy lines on the Patchwork Diagram. First sew 5 light As and 5 dark As together in unmatched pairs along the long edges to form square units. Stitch them into rows as shown; then stitch the rows together. Stitch the second-to-longest edge of D to the pieced sections. Join a light A with a B and a C to form the corner square. Stitch this square to the smaller unit, which includes a D patch; then sew the 2 sections together.

- ❖ **Sewing the Appliqué:** Stay-stitch just outside the stitching line along E's curves. Clip into the seam allowances and press them to the wrong side. (It may be it helpful to center the template on the wrong side of E and press the seam allowances over the cardboard edges.) Place E on F, with the raw edges even and the handle ends equally distanced from the corners; appliqué first along the inside curve, then along the outside curve.

- ❖ **Making the Flowers:** Refer to the actual-size patterns on page 197. (You may prefer to fill the baskets with the same contents or use different floral designs, as shown on this quilt.) Use the patterns as a general guide for scale. Draw some leaves and flower shapes freehand on various scraps of fabric. Cut them out and appliqué them onto F. Use 2 or 3 strands of embroidery floss in an embroidery needle to chain-stitch or backstitch the stems, stamens, or other

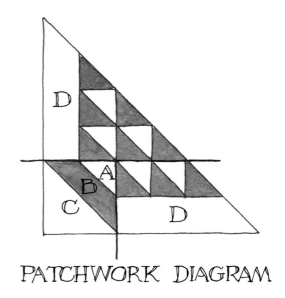

PATCHWORK DIAGRAM

lines and to satin-stitch petals, calyses, or other larger areas. For small, circular flowers, berries, or buds, make yo-yos as follows: Cut out a fabric circle just over 2 times the size of the desired finished yo-yo. Thread a needle and knot the 2 ends of the thread together. Turn under a ⅛" (0.3 cm) hem to the wrong side of the circle and sew the hem all around with small running stitches. Gather the thread up tightly and finish off by backstitching inconspicuously 2 or 3 times. Press the yo-yo. Pin the yo-yo to F with either side showing, and appliqué all around its edges to secure it in place.

Stitch the patchwork triangle to F along the longest edges; the finished block should measure 9" (22.9 cm) within seam allowances.

- ❖ **Assembling the Quilt Top:** Place each light lattice strip between 2 dark lattice strips and stitch along their long edges to form a striped lattice sash. Referring to the photograph, arrange the quilt top on a large surface: Place the blocks in 6 rows of 6, leaving 5" between blocks. Turn the baskets on the left and right halves so they all face the center, as shown. Place the lattice sashes in the spaces between the blocks and around the outer edges of the quilt top. Place a lattice square at each intersection of the lattice sashes. Stitch the quilt blocks, lattice sashes, and lattice squares into horizontal rows. Then stitch the rows together, taking care to match the seams. Add a light and then a dark heading strip at the top edge of the quilt top.

- ❖ **Assembling the Quilt:** Mark the quilt top for quilting. This quilt features standard quilting on the A and B patches; a simple 4-petal posy on each lattice square; parallel diagonal lines of quilting over the C and D patches, the lattice sashes, and the heading; and contour or echo quilting on the F patches. Cut and piece the backing. Cut the batting and baste the layers together.

- ❖ **Finishing:** Quilt as marked or as desired. Make a binding from dark fabric and attach it all around.

QUILT BLOCK DIAGRAM

To define a stair landing, the owners hung a Trip Around the World quilt on the wall and casually folded another over an old wooden apple-picking ladder (above). A stairwell is the perfect place to show off favorite quilts; there is usually a banister just waiting to be draped. In a log cabin in Door County, Wisconsin (left), a pair of Log Cabin quilts in Straight Furrow arrangements are laid over handcrafted cedar railings to extend a cheery greeting to all who pass by. An oddly shaped space in an upstairs stairwell (opposite) was transformed into an art gallery when its owners opted to hang quilts there.

Decorating with Quilts

Quilts have never really left the common rooms of the house. If the quilting bee of yesteryear could not be held outdoors because of inclement weather, a living room or great room was used. On other days, a woman would most likely sew there alone, relishing both the light and warmth of a fire. Today, these rooms, devoted to relaxation and entertainment, provide an excellent arena in which to display treasured handmade textiles.

Because of quilts' strong graphic quality, they fall somewhere between furniture and accessories. They are, in fact, a powerful decorating tool. Simply because of their size, quilts have a way of dominating a room, so they need to be placed artfully. Either they can establish the whole tone and color scheme of a room through the impact of their bold designs and dramatic colors, or they can act as more subtle, versatile accents. It helps to determine the type of role a quilt is to play in an overall decorating scheme, carefully considering the particular graphic pattern, its color, and its contrasts with other objects in the room.

Decorating with quilts in living rooms can take many forms. All it requires is some ingenuity and a little experimentation. The couch is a good place to start. The back can be an easel of sorts. It is possible to drape a quilt over it, then lay a contrasting one casually over a nearby chair.

Framed quilts look dramatic, especially hung over a mantelpiece. A spotlight, complete with an ultraviolet filter to protect the fabric, helps show off the delicate stitching. Depending on the texture and color of a quilt, it can function as a backdrop for other objects.

Quilts can also make intriguing window treatments. A quilt scrap, folded in a triangle, can be tacked up by two

The stark simplicity of this city apartment (above) is warmed by a variety of needlework. Bear's Paw and One-Patch pillows decorate the sofa where a Double Irish Chain quilt is displayed. An antique sampler hangs above the mantel. Pillows made from coverlet pieces grace the wing chair and the child's chair by the fire. In the living room of a Connecticut farmhouse

(opposite) prints and graphics of fabrics and quilts come to life against an all-white background. A Nine-Patch crib quilt hangs over the sofa, framed by a sawtooth border. A Compass Star quilt beckons from the arm of the sofa. A rusty braided rug adds subtle color and texture to the floor.

corners over a window so that it hangs down like a hand-kerchief. Topping three windows with three different quilt scraps provides an even more original look.

It may be necessary to take a break from quilts once in a while. For those times when a sparer look is in order, quilts can be folded or put away for a needed rest. When they come out of hiding again, they can be enjoyed all the more.

This vivid Star pattern, created with four high-contrast colors, dominates a country living room (above). Eight smaller stars circling the one in the center add to the quilt's drama.

110

A shipshape Connecticut cottage (right) with a ticking-covered armchair is cheered by a Nine-Patch variation quilt with Broken Dishes corner blocks, circa 1890–1900. The quilt's graphic look is accented by a handpainted checkerboard floor. It looks like pure New England (previous page), but this saltbox house, circa 1980, was built in Florida by native Kentuckians with country in their hearts. The living room sofa is covered with six- and eight-pointed Stars quilts, in true New England style.

Strip-Patchwork Crib Quilt

DIRECTIONS

❖ **Notes:** Read over the Quiltmaking Basics and refer to them throughout. Remember to add seam allowances to all dimensions.

❖ **Piecing Strips:** Mark and cut 2" (5.1 cm) strips across the entire width of each fabric: 4 from the dark fabric and 8 from the light. Stitch a dark strip between 2 light strips as shown in Figure 1. Also refer to Figure 1 to cut across the joined strips at intervals to make 66 segments 2" x 6" (5.1 x 15.2 cm), plus seam allowance all around. Stagger these segments as shown in Figure 2, and stitch them together into 6 rows of 11, taking care to match corners of dark squares.

On the wrong side, mark a stitching line through the top and bottom corners of the dark squares (see Figure 3). Cut off the points of light squares, leaving the width of a seam allowance beyond the marked line.

❖ **Assembling the Quilt Top:** From the dark fabric, cut 7 strips 1 ¾" x 30" (4.5 x 76.2 cm). Arrange alternating dark and pieced strips in horizontal rows, starting and ending with a dark strip. You may wish to stagger or line up the dark squares from row to row. Pin, then stitch the rows together, following the marked lines on the pieced strips to ensure sharp points on the top and bottom corners of the dark squares. Trim the edges of the quilt top into a neat rectangle.

❖ **Assembling the Quilt:** Mark a quilting design on the quilt top. Cut out backing and batting and baste the layers together.

❖ **Finishing:** Quilt along marked lines or ⅛" (0.3 cm) from seams; it is also feasible to tie this quilt. Make a binding with the dark fabric and attach it all around.

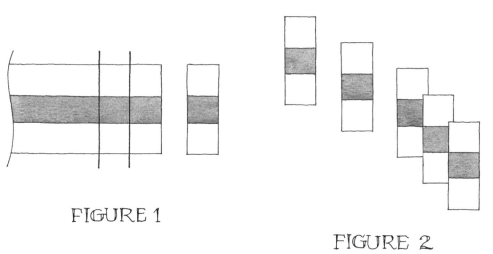

FIGURE 1

FIGURE 2

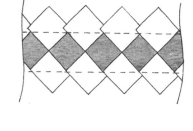

FIGURE 3

119

A Room for Broken Dishes and a Wild Goose Chase

A winning menu for decorating a country dining room may well include quilts. They can be rotated with the seasons or reserved for special meals, celebrations, and family gatherings. A birthday, anniversary, or holiday like Christmas or Passover might be an ideal occasion for displaying fine handmade textiles.

Choosing patterns appropriate for a room devoted to feasting and food can lead to amusing motifs. Designs such as Broken Dishes, Drunkard's Path, and Wild Goose Chase are a few possibilities. A dining room with a fireplace provides the right setting for a Log Cabin quilt, with its center square of red representing a hearth.

Quilts can provide padding in a room that tends to be heavy on wood. Quilts are also powerful symbols of warmth and security, filling psychological needs as well as contributing tactile pleasures so welcome in a dining room. One decorating idea is to dress up plain ladderback chairs with slipcovers made from quilt tops stitched pillowcase-style. Another unusual effect is achieved in a simple Shaker-style dining room: The owner sometimes secures a loop of ribbon on a peg rack, which circles the room at eye level, and pulls one corner of a quilt through the loop, spreading out the bottom to show off the design. A similar idea is applied in an old English farmhouse where the dining room's nonworking fireplace is swagged with a quilt hanging from loops of decorative cording attached to the mantelpiece and tied in big bows.

The whole idea of using quilts in a dining room, however, is controversial. New York decorator Woody Goldfein, who loves to work with quilts, says he cringes when he sees magazine photographs of berries and cream served on a quilt (see The Great Tabletop Controversy on page 127). He and his family love to live with their quilts, enjoying them in everyday life, but he warns that they must be treated with great care. Designer Gerald Roy in Oakland, California, cautions that any coverlet with historic or sentimental value has no place in a dining room where it can absorb odors and moisture and can be ruined by candle wax or food stains.

If a quilt in a dining room would achieve a desired effect but the use of an actual piece is out of the question, there are interesting alternatives. Plain muslin curtains can be stenciled with a quilt motif along the lower edge. Or a heavy canvas floorcloth can be painted in a quilt pattern with acrylic paints, well protected with several coats of a nonyellowing sealer. Designs that attract the eye by creating optical illusions or three-dimensional effects, such as Bow Tie, Tumbling Blocks, or particular Log Cabin variations, can also be stenciled in a frieze bordering the room.

A dining room quilt often functions as a backdrop, injecting large areas of pattern and color into an otherwise plain space. In this dining room (opposite), the honeyed tones of the sideboard, hutch, and table are accented by a Baby Blocks quilt on the wall. That design requires an experienced quilter who can manipulate solid and calico squares to create the illusion of depth and movement. The quilt acts as a frame for a collection of willowware plates on the sideboard. The lantern is an effective accessory here; the quilt can be seen through it. An appliqué quilt makes a wooden bench more comfortable.

The Great Tabletop Controversy

The jury is still out on whether to use a quilt as table linen. Authorities agree that valuable or antique quilts should never be used, especially if there is a risk of spills from food and drink. One solution is to place a quilt under glass, protecting it from spills, dust, and stains. However, some experts counter that glass masks its tactile, three-dimensional aspect, which is one of the special qualities that make quilts so attractive, and that glass cannot protect it from odors. Of course, no quilt should stay under glass for an extended period of time, as this will hasten the breakdown of its fibers.

One way to get around this dilemma is to make a quilt specifically for use on the table, then treat it in the same manner as any other fine table linen. Quilts made of fabric that is easily washable or that has been treated with a protectant such as Scotchguard™ can lend a festive and dramatic air to a dining table, and the confident hostess knows she doesn't have to worry about an occasional accident.

Another way to use a quilt on a dining table is as a special treat. In the sunroom of an Illinois log home (opposite), the breakfast table is set with a patchwork and appliqué Ohio Stars quilt the owners found at a church rummage sale. Knowing it is not destined for a museum, the family feels free to use it on special occasions, with placemats for added protection.

A quilt sometimes makes a wonderful display when draped on a more out-of-the-way table.

Rather than dominating a room, the Broken Star quilt with a pink sawtooth border and small radiant stars in the corners (above) tops a side table. It has been cushioned by a floor-sweeping underskirt of cotton.

One precaution when using a quilt on any table is to place a table pad under it. This protects the fabric from direct contact with the wood surface, whose oils might stain it over time.

Cats of all kinds abound in the dining room of an old house in St. Louis, Missouri (left). Felines play on the Cactus Basket quilt that adorns the long harvest table. The grain-painted sideboard from Indiana is another refuge for cats, while still others are permanently situated in the hooked rug on the stairway wall. An Arizona adobe house can boast a country look (above). In this dining-room corner, a One-Patch Checkerboard crib quilt graces the edge of a nineteenthth-century hutch topped by a running-horse weathervane. Amish bonnets, graduated boxes, and an Amish farm rake are silhouetted against stark white walls. A colorful Stars quilt that was handmade by its owner hangs near the window of a Vermont dining room (opposite). A local craftsman made the table from the top of an old grain box; a 1920s hooked rug covers the floor.

Simplicity reigns in the wide-open great room of a secluded Pennsylvania farmhouse (left). The owners employ quilts as exclamation points against the basic blue-and-white surroundings of their living and dining areas. A School-house quilt holds forth from the back of a Shaker bench. Near the fieldstone fireplace, red-and-white quilts are folded over the sofas; the one on the left is an Irish Chain. Hand-hewn beams salvaged from a barn in New York State take the place of a bearing wall and allow the room to stretch over forty feet to an open kitchen behind the dining table. This entire wing was added to the house during renovation; the owners made sure to include lots of windows to bring in the great outdoors.

Framed Medallion Quilt

> **THE ESSENTIALS**
>
> **FINISHED SIZE**
>
> 39 ¼" (99.7 cm) square
>
> •
>
> **MATERIALS**
>
> 1 ¼ yards (1.1 m) for the backing
>
> •
>
> ¾ yard (68.6 cm) each of Fabric 1
> (here, off-white), Fabric 2 (here,
> olive), and Fabric 3 (here, black) for
> backgrounds, borders, patches, and
> appliqués, plus small amounts of
> assorted fabrics for patches
>
> •
>
> White sewing and quilting thread
>
> •
>
> Batting
>
> •
>
> Additional supplies as listed in the
> Quiltmaking Basics on page 185

DIRECTIONS

❖ **Notes:** This small quilt incorporates both patchwork and appliqué techniques and embellishes them with an array of quilting patterns.

Read the Quiltmaking Basics and refer to them throughout. Remember that seam allowances must be added when cutting all pieces.

❖ **Preparing Patterns and Templates:** Use the actual-size patterns on page 198 to make templates for B, C, D, and E. Then make a complete pattern for A from tracing paper.

❖ **Making the Medallion:** From Fabric 1, cut a 14" (35.6 cm) square for the medallion background. Use the templates to cut 1 A and 8 B from Fabric 1 and 8 C from Fabric 2.

Fold the background and A in half diagonally in both directions and press to crease the fold lines; then unfold them. Use dressmaker's tracing (carbon) paper to transfer quilting lines, as indicated by the dotted lines, on to each quadrant. Center A on the background, matching the creases, and pin. Place 2 B patches within each quadrant so that circle A overlaps each of their slightly curved edges by 2 seam allowance widths. Place a C in between all B pieces; refer to the pattern for placement. Appliqué all overlapping edges to the background. Cut 4 strips ⅝" x 15 ¼" (1.6 x 38.7 cm). Stitch 1 to each side of the background square, mitering the corners.

❖ **Making the Medallion Corners:** Make a pattern for the triangle that results when a 10 ⅞" (27.6 cm) square is cut diagonally in half. Use it to cut 4 triangles from Fabric 3. Use the template for D to cut 48 diamond-shaped patches. Arrange them on the long edge of each corner triangle, as shown in Figure 2. Stitch them into units of 3, as indicated by the heavy lines in Figure 2. Stitch the units together in pairs, taking care to match the diamond points; then stitch the pairs together. Press the triangle in half and pin the patchwork on to the triangle so that the raw edges are even and the center seam is along the crease. Turn under those edges of the

FIGURE 1 . MEDALLION

FIGURE 2 . MEDALLION CORNERS

outside diamonds not along the raw edge, and appliqué. Pin and stitch one triangle to each side of the center square, forming a larger square. Cut 4 strips 1" x 23¾" (2.5 x 60.3 cm) from Fabric 2. Stitch 1 to each edge of the medallion, mitering the corners.

❖ **Sewing the Diamond Borders:** From Fabric 2, cut 4 rectangles 6¾" x 23¾" (17.2 x 60.3 cm) for side borders. From Fabric 3, cut 4 pieces 6¾" (17.1 cm) square for the corner blocks.

❖ **Making the Side Borders:** Use the template for diamond E to mark and cut 56 patches from Fabric 1, 8 from another fabric, and 16 each from 3 other fabrics (do not use Fabric 2). Position 4 diamonds together as shown in Figure 3. Stitch them together in pairs; then stitch the pairs together, taking care to match the diamond points. Turn the seam allowance along the outer edges to the wrong side and press. You will have 4 of 1 color combination (joined diamond I). Similarly, make 8 of 3 other color combinations (joined diamonds II, III, and IV). Pin 7 of these joined diamonds along each side border in the following sequence: IV, III, II, I, II, III, IV. Ease joined diamonds to fit between the seam allowances. Appliqué around each joined diamond.

❖ **Piecing the Corner Blocks:** Use template D to mark and cut 16 diamonds from Fabric 1 and 16 from other assorted fabrics. Alternate 4 white and 4 patches of other colors on the background square as shown in Figure 4. Referring to the heavy lines in Figure 4, stitch the diamonds together in pairs; then stitch 2 adjacent pairs together; and lastly, stitch the halves together to form a complete star. Center the star on the corner block, press under the outer edges, and appliqué in place.

Join 2 borders to opposite sides of the medallion. Stitch a corner block to either end of the 2 remaining sides. Stitch these to the remaining sides of the medallion, taking care to match the seams.

❖ **Sewing the Plain Border:** Cut 4 strips 1" x 39¼" (2.5 x 99.7 cm), or the length needed to match each side of the quilt top so far, plus 2" (5.1 cm). Stitch a strip, which is centered, to each side. Miter the corners.

❖ **Assembling the Quilt:** Mark the quilt top for quilting as desired. Cut the backing and the batting and baste them together.

❖ **Finishing:** To duplicate the quilting on the piece shown, follow the marked lines on circle A. Stitch ⅛" (0.3 cm) to the inside on A, B, C, and E patches

FIGURE 3

FIGURE 4

and appliqués. Quilt the medallion center background in lines ⅜" (1.0 cm) apart, radiating outward within each quadrant. Quilt in the ditch along all D patches and along the thin border strips. Work in narrow echo quilting over the triangular areas of the border strips between the joined diamonds.

Make a binding from Fabric 2 and attach it all around.

Uncommon Rooms for Quilts

Though cooking with quilts around might seem like a recipe for success, quilt lovers face a quandry when using them in a kitchen. Humidity, heat, and sunshine can wreak havoc with quilts, and kitchens and baths usually contain all three in abundance. That is why quilt experts unanimously agree that kitchens and baths are not the right places for precious textiles. They particularly caution against storing quilts in a bathroom linen closet or using any nineteenth-century bed coverings in these rooms because of their fragile nature. Quilts of more recent vintage that are deemed less valuable may serve a valid decorating purpose and provide the same color and graphic interest as older items. They can be used judiciously in kitchens and baths and be quite beautiful there.

One solution might be to buy a new work and use it like a new tablecloth or shower curtain, expecting that it will become worn with time and have to be discarded. The newest all-cotton quilts are made in China, have lots of quilting stitches, and are filled with cotton batting so they look old. These quilts can live in a kitchen or bath,

and there is no risk of ruining a priceless antique. Fragments of old counterpanes too far gone for any other purpose ~ often called "cutter quilts" ~ can also be used. Another solution is to machine-sew a quilt top and backing using polyester fabrics and fill it with polyester batting. That way it is machine-washable and can be treated like any easy-care blanket.

Quilt tops and blocks, often found at quilting fairs, festivals, and conferences (see Resources on page 204 for listings), are another source of decorative material. Through the years, many quilt tops were never finished with batting and backing. Maybe their makers made far more than they could actually use, or some might be considered inferior work. Those stitched during the twentieth century are still plentiful and affordable. They can be used in kitchens or baths without worry that a valuable piece of history is being destroyed.

Decorating with quilt pieces is the easiest way to use textiles in the kitchen. Quilted blocks or strips laid side by side on a stretch of open shelves, their pointed ends down like handkerchiefs, can show off pretty bowls, plates, or other kitchen collectibles, much as a doily shows off a party cake.

Of course, quilts that are only seen from the kitchen will be protected from the worst of kitchen perils. For instance, the wall of a sitting room that opens on a kitchen might be the best place to hang a brilliant Star of Bethlehem quilt. Then take color inspiration from the quilt and have tiles made for kitchen countertops and a backsplash depicting different star motifs. The effect is cheering and at the same time it unifies the room in an imaginative way. Such is the power of quilts.

The brilliant colors of a hand-stitched Amish Sunshine and Shadows crib quilt give a warm focus to the keeping room in a 1740s clapboard house in Virginia (opposite). The original cooking quarters were outdoors, so the new owners, who bought the house at auction, decided to fashion a kitchen and keeping room in the old brick basement. Far from gloomy, this new heart of the house boasts a working fireplace, a painted North Carolina table, and a portion of the owners' basket and crock collection in a hutch from the Shenandoah Valley.

In Texas, a Lone Star quilt gets its just display folded on the back of an old wooden settle (left). On the wall above is another example of superb needlework ~ a sampler dated 1877. Draping the kitchen table (above), a Straight Furrows variation of a Log Cabin quilt lends its lively colors and pattern to a summer luncheon. A Bow Ties quilt top, found unfinished at an antiques show, makes an original shower curtain in a city apartment where country reigns supreme (opposite). Buttonholes were stitched across the top to accommodate curtain hooks and a plastic liner was added. In the hall-way, an antique apple-picking ladder provides access to out-of-reach books and baskets stored overhead.

Quilts on Porches

Putting quilts on porches often causes quilt dealers and restorers to shudder a little. Most experts believe that if a quilt is left on a porch, its owner should be prepared for it to fade very quickly. However, if a favorite counterpane is already faded, it may as well bring pleasure to those who relax on the porch. After all, a faded cotton sundress has its own special beauty and nostalgic quality.

The owner of this Texas farm-house leaves her furniture on the porch no matter what the weather, though she waits to bring out her favorite quilts until guests arrive. For a special lunch (above), a striking Ocean Waves quilt decorates a New Jersey chair table. Since willow and log furniture is not neces-sarily the most comfortable, the owners of a weekend house in the Berkshires (opposite) rely on

their collection of quilt-patch pillows and lengths of sturdy blue denim fabric to cushion the seats on their screened porch. Some of the pillows are made from Churn Dash and Triangle quilt blocks; others are covered in blue-and-white ticking like the covering of long-ago country mattresses. To make sure they last, the pillows and fabric are stored in a closet during the week.

Placing a quilt only on a deep, well-protected porch ~ never in a sunroom or on an open patio ~ is one precau-tion owners can consider. Another is always to bring the piece inside after it is used, especially during a rainstorm. The walls of a porch are often large enough to support a hanging quilt. Either make one especially for this purpose, preferably with polyester fabrics, or pick one that is already faded. In a woodsy setting, it might be interesting to echo the colors of the surrounding acreage, perhaps making hangings to rotate with the seasons. A bucolic scene or animal motifs such as butterflies, sheep, or even elephants will promote a country feeling in a city setting.

Certain quilt patterns with themes that center on nature are ideal for porches: flower baskets, windmill blades, stars, grapevines, feathers. Even the names of quilt patterns have a special affinity with the outdoors ~ Pine Tree, Log Cabin, Ocean Waves. A lot of nature's bounty is depicted in quilts. Perhaps that is why they look so natural when they appear outside.

A table with a Log Cabin quilt and an underskirt of pink cotton makes a pretty oasis on the open porch of a log house in the woods (left). The tapestry pillow on the antique wicker rocker is part of a larger collection displayed indoors. This back porch (above) is the open-air studio of a Montana painter, whose collection of quilts is apt to be called into play for impromtu still-life compositions. This one includes a Nine-Patch quilt, an old decoy, and flowers from her garden.

Personal Touches for A Rented Home

When America's pioneer women packed their wagons with all their worldly goods and set off for parts unknown, taking along their quilts was hardly a matter of decorating. Quilts were needed to keep the family warm during the westward journey; when the family settled, they covered beds and shaded windows in new sod houses or log cabins. Traveling with quilts today still carries a sense of adventure and opportunity, but threats to survival are not the same when packing up the station wagon and heading off to a summer house with a load of quilts.

A brass bed's Hawaiian-style appliqué quilt and flannel sheets are not just pretty - they are practical necessities at an Illinois log lodge deep in the woods (opposite). Even in summer, nights are cold here. The thick rug underfoot helps, as does a buffalo plaid blanket stowed in a basket. Embroidered tea towels on the bedside table take the place of a napkin and place-mat beneath a warming cup of tea. The antique oak high chair on wheels has been in the lodge for as long as anyone can remember. A parade of geraniums thrive in stenciled wooden buckets on the latticed radiator covers, accenting the colors in the room.

Quilts can give a rental house a personal stamp. One New York family rents the same Connecticut house each summer. They always arrive with their favorite quilts, lamps, pottery, picture frames, and books in tow. The first day is spent personalizing the interior. Their own treasures are spread about, and all the things they don't like are put in boxes, which are piled in an extra bedroom and covered with a quilt. The old beige sofa is draped with quilts for a loose slipcovered effect; one work is laid on the seat, another on the back, so there is no pulling on the textiles when someone is sitting. An ottoman and a funny-looking end table in a corner are always disguised with pieced toppings. Small framed quilt blocks decorate the walls. The transformation gives the house a new and personal look for the entire summer.

Quilts look different in new settings. Displaying them in a summer house or winter retreat allows them to be seen in a whole new light. In fact, the quality of the light may be noticeably different in the mountains or at the seashore than it is at home. With different colors around them, in rooms with different exposures, quilts can take on a fresh appearance.

145

There is a cozy quilt virtually everywhere in this Long Island summer house (left and above). A hand-me-down sofa is disguised with pastel pillows and a Letter H quilt over its cushions. The Album quilt laid over the ottoman belonged to a long-ago ancestor; each square is signed in the center. In the cozy sleeping loft (above), a bright Bear's Paw quilt adds interest. This charming house served generations of youngsters as a playhouse on the grounds of a rambling estate before being converted to a snug cottage for grown-ups. During the conversion, space was gained by adding the loft. Thick timbers make the loft look as if it has always been part of the house.

A Whig Rose quilt, made in Lambs, Pennsylvania, tops a four-poster rope bed in the old-fashioned living room of a Texas farmhouse (left). Originally the farmhouse was an inn, and it still retains some of the rare ornamental painting done by a German immigrant artist during its construction in the nineteenthth century.

Antique or heirloom quilts require special care and must be carefully handled and displayed. Even the oil from a person's hands can hasten the deterioration of a precious piece, so curators often wear thin cotton gloves when handling vintage textiles. Because of the effects of age, the fibers of old quilts are already weakened and the colors are faded. There may also be holes, tears, or worn spots.

Always put the cleaning and repair of such quilts into expert hands. Even if an antique quilt does seem strong enough for display, it is best to keep it out only for a few months, then put it away to rest for an equal period of time. Rotating quilts this way will help prevent further damage, although nothing can stop it entirely.

Under no circumstances should a fragile quilt be used on a bed. It cannot withstand the tugging, pulling, and tucking that is part of every bedding routine. Light and heat are particular enemies of these delicate textiles. Never keep an old quilt folded in one position for very long; it is a good practice to refold it at least every six months or less.

A two-color decorating theme is an easy way to achieve harmony in any room. Blue and white have been chosen for the living room of this renovated log cabin in Ohio (right). White plaster walls are a stark backdrop for the geometric patterns of the patchwork quilts that rest over the poplar banister overhead. A darker quilt drapes the wing chair in the foreground. The quilts' blue tones are echoed by sofa pillows made from coverlet pieces and by the antique Canton porcelain that lines the mantel. The two-story fireplace was built of stones from the backyard creek.

A cat stitched from quilt scraps (right) keeps watch over a basket of crib quilts and unfinished quilt blocks that may someday be sewn into pillows, seat covers, or more cats. The child's ladderback chair is a perfect throne for a tiny rag doll and her crib quilt. When a quilt collection grows and grows, whole rooms are sometimes devoted to show- ing it off (opposite). This table is a veritable still life, display- ing one collector's many passions. First and foremost are quilts by the dozen ~ some old, some new. Patchwork pillows and stuffed animals made from quilt pieces are another consuming interest. Scattered baskets, flowers, a decoy, and a chair hanging from the rafters complete the country tableau.

Quilts as Wall Hangings

Moving a quilt from the bed to the wall can elevate a humble textile to a powerful piece of art. Since quilts come in so many styles, shapes, sizes, colors, and patterns, they run the gamut from homey folk art to majestic abstract statements. Treating a quilt as fine art serves to protect a valuable investment.

In general, do not do anything to a quilt that cannot be undone; any repair or restoration should be reversible. In fact, it is a good practice to keep a detailed record of any work that is performed.

A quilt destined for a wall must be sturdy enough to withstand the stress of hanging. Attaching loops or a casing may add wear and tear. Remember that a quilt should not come in direct contact with any wooden support or hanger, as the natural oils in the wood can stain the fabric. Instead, seal the wood with polyurethane varnish or cover it with acid-free paper. Never enclose a quilt in a completely sealed frame; it needs to breathe.

Textile experts recommend the following methods for hanging quilts:

The quilt in this Nebraska living room (opposite) dates from the 1920s, a particularly prolific period in American quiltmaking. The back of the quilt has a casing sewn across its top edge so a wooden pole can be slipped through; the pole is then hung from wooden brackets, just as a curtain would be.

❖ Velcro™. A hidden method of hanging lightweight quilts is to use strips of Velcro ~ one attached to the quilt, the other to a strip on the wall. This is the preferred method of hanging antique quilts and is the method often chosen by collectors who rotate their quilts frequently. Velcro can also be attached to battens suspended from the ceiling with pulleys and nylon yachting cord, so quilts can be used as room dividers, suspended as canopies, or hung as free-floating artwork in large, loftlike spaces.

To create these strips, cut the Velcro slightly shorter than the quilt width. Cut two fabric strips the same length and about two inches wide. Machine-stitch the Velcro to the fabric strips. Attach the strips to the quilt by using an overcast stitch all around the fabric, sewing through the backing to the padding for extra support. Glue or staple the other fabric strip to the support bar and attach to the wall (or to battens, as mentioned above). Press the two Velcro strips together to hang the quilt.

❖ Hanging Sleeves or Casing. Another hidden method is to attach several sleeves or one long casing (depending on the size of the work) to the back of a quilt. Sewing a casing along each edge of the quilt back allows it to be hung from a different edge each time, which minimizes any stretching effects and increases the life of the quilt.

Cut the casing about one inch longer than the width of the quilt and about eight inches deep. Fold it in half lengthwise and sew it along the long edge. Turn the right

side out and press the casing with a seam in the center of one side. Turn in the raw edges and stitch. Slip-stitch the casing's top and bottom edges to the back of the quilt. Insert a wood or metal pole, strip, or dowel, and hang that on the wall. The rod holder can be completely hidden or can have decorative finials.

❖ Hanging Loops. A series of loops stitched across the top of a quilt is a decorative method of attaching a quilt to a rod, dowel, or wood strip. Cut some fabric strips twice the desired width and long enough to go around the pole and overlap on to the quilt about one inch. Cut enough strips so they can be spaced evenly across the quilt, leaving about two inches of space between the strips. Fold each strip in half lengthwise, and sew it along the long length. Turn the right side out, iron it with the seam at the center of one side, fold it in half, and turn the raw edges inward. Sew the loops to the top edge of the quilt back. Insert the pole and suspend the ends from wall- or ceiling-mounted brackets or from wire or hooks on the wall or ceiling.

❖ Mounting on a Stretcher. Purchase a wooden stretcher, slightly larger than the quilt, from a framing or craft shop. Seal the wood using polyurethane varnish, or wrap the stretcher with acid-free tissue paper. Choose silk, cotton, or linen mounting cloth, wrap it around the stretcher, and secure it to the back using rustproof staples or brass tacks. Position the quilt on the cloth, pin it in place, and secure it with a running blind hem stitch. The mounting

Bold Amish and Mennonite quilts are in striking contrast to their makers' quiet, down-to-earth lives. Stitched with skill and imagination, these quilts are functional masterpieces. What makes them so compelling? Without doubt, it is their strong abstract patterns, which evolved because these plain people were forbidden by their religion to use naturalist motifs. The Amish-like simplicity of a bedroom in a Bethlehem, Pennsylvania, mill house (left) focuses attention on the wool Log Cabin quilt on the wall. It was made in the Amish and Mennonite community of Lahaska, Pennsylvania, in the 1920s. The owners built and painted the pencil-post bed themselves.

cloth makes a decorative border around the quilt. Hang the stretcher on the wall with picture wire and hooks.

❖ Hanging Systems. For professional-quality mounting at home, use textile hanging devices such as the Walker System. Any kind of unmounted textile can be hung using a combination of the system's metal bars, rods, or clips and wall-mounted brackets. There is no need for stretcher mounts, and it is easy to change quilts on display. The system is also used in many galleries and museums across the country.

The two most common methods of hanging quilts with such systems include from a bar faced with Velcro hook tape, which is ready to accept the matching loop tape sewn to the back of the textile, or from a fabric sleeve that suspends the textile from a metal rod. Lighter textiles or fragments can be displayed from clips attached to rods mounted on the wall.

Think creatively when it comes to hanging supports for quilts. Instead of dowels, use decorative or turned wood poles or curtain rods. Consider metal rather than wood, or even try tree branches for a primitive look. Decorate the ends of hangers with finials, tassels, dried flowers, ribbons, or bows.

In the process of salvaging a nineteenth-century frame house in northwest Florida, the restorers discovered hooks on the front-room ceiling (left). Puzzled but determined to preserve the original flavor of the pioneer home, they set about interviewing local residents. They discovered that several elderly women in the region remembered attending quilting bees there. It seems a quilt in a frame was lowered from the ceiling so the women could work on it. Though the owners opted to suspend their quilt with the design facing down, their unique way of displaying a quilt is true to the house. In a log house in Ohio (following page), a Country Lanes quilt hung behind a three-quarter bed creates drama in an otherwise plain room. (Directions for making this Country Lanes quilt are on pages 168-169.)

Country Lanes Quilt

DIRECTIONS

❖ **Note:** Read over the Quiltmaking Basics and refer to them throughout. Remember that seam allowances must be added when cutting all pieces.

❖ **Preparing Templates:** Make templates as follows: A is a 2 ½" (6.4 cm) square, B is a 1 ¼" (3.2 cm) square, C is a 1 ¼" x 2 ½" (3.2 x 6.4 cm) rectangle, D is a 1 ¼ " x 5" (3.2 x 12.7 cm) rectangle, and a plain block that is 7 ½" (19.1 cm) square.

❖ **Cutting Borders:** Cut the outer borders from Fabric 1: 2 strips 10" x 86" (25.4 x 218.4 cm) and 2 strips 10" x 96" (25.4 x 243.8 cm). Cut the inner borders from Fabric 2: 2 strips 4" x 66" (10.2 x 167.6 cm) and 2 strips 4" x 76" (10.2 x 193.0 cm). Set these aside.

❖ **Cutting Patches:** Use the template for the plain block to cut 42 blocks from Fabric 1. Use the other templates to cut 30 A and 120 B from Fabric 2, 120 C from Fabric 3, 120 D from Fabric 4, and 120 B from Fabric 5.

❖ **Making Each Block:** Make an inner 9-patch block as follows: Arrange the patches as shown in Figure 1. Refer to the Fabric Key. Stitch the patches together in horizontal rows, then stitch the rows together, taking care to match the seams for sharp corners.

Frame each inner 9-patch block as shown in Figure 2: First, stitch a D patch to 2 opposite sides of a 9-patch. Stitch a B to either end of 2 more D patches and stitch the joined B-D-B piece to the remaining sides of the block. Repeat to make a total of 30 framed 9-patch blocks.

❖ **Assembling the Quilt Top:** Arrange the pieced blocks and plain blocks following the Assembly Diagram. Stitch them together in horizontal rows, then stitch the rows together, taking care to match the seams. Add the inner, then the outer borders as follows: Stitch the long strips to the long edges of the quilt top; then trim the ends even with the quilt top edges at the top and bottom. Stitch the shorter strips to the top and the bottom of the quilt; trim the ends even with the side borders.

❖ **Assembling the Quilt:** Mark a quilting design on the quilt top. Here, the pieced blocks are quilted in a diagonal grid. A circular wreath is used in the center of each block, and a narrow and wide chain link design is used for the inner and outer borders, respectively.

❖ **Finishing:** Cut the backing and the batting and baste the layers together. Quilt as marked. Make a binding from Fabric 3 and attach it all around.

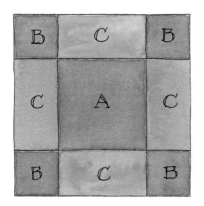

FIGURE 1

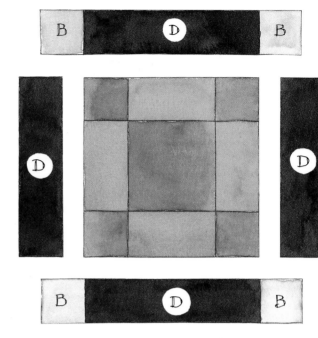

FIGURE 2

FABRIC KEY

= FABRIC 3

= FABRIC 1

= FABRIC 4

= FABRIC 2

= FABRIC 5

ASSEMBLY DIAGRAM

ROW 1
ROW 2
ROW 3

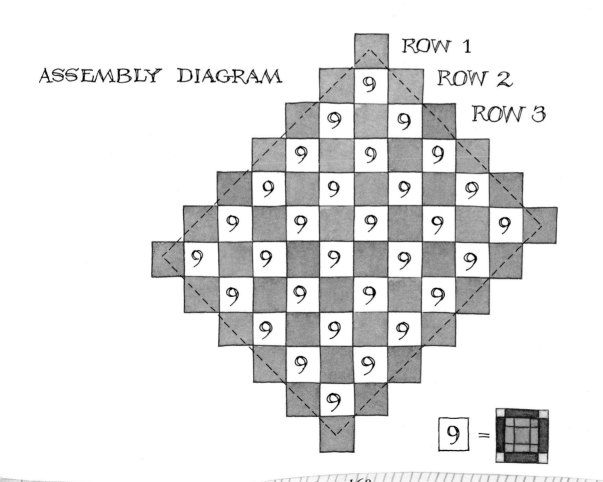

9 =

An Ocean Waves quilt gives this sitting room the airy freshness that the combination of blue and white provides (above). The sofa's classic country checks are a perfect pairing with the wall hangings. The quilt is hung from binder clips, which can be found at stationery stores. Each clip has two tabs that open; one is folded down over the quilt, the other is hung from a nail in the wall. The clips are evenly placed across the entire top edge of the quilt and are moved several inches one way or the other every few months to protect the fabric. An 1840s Indiana log home (opposite) was transferred piece by piece from the field of an Amish farmer. It still shows its Amish provenance in the quilts that decorate the bedroom. A 1910 Ocean Waves quilt splashes vivid Amish geometry on the wall. (Directions for making this Ocean Waves quilt are on pages 172–175.) Bedcovers include a 1925 Amish Pinwheel quilt, a folded 1915 Courthouse Steps quilt, and a fringed homespun blanket.

Ocean Waves Quilt

DIRECTIONS

❖ **Notes:** In these directions, the fabric amounts and the number of pieces to be cut from each fabric are based on the arrangement of colors in the quilt shown. To redesign the colors, use the Color-It-Yourself Quilt Top Diagram. Simply photocopy the chart and fill it in with colored pencils.

In the quilt shown, some of the light blue fabric has faded to gray; all this material is referred to as Fabric 3.

The quilt shown is hand-pieced, with prism-shaped sections sewn around A squares. Their short sides are joined, then corner B and side C pieces are set in. For an experienced quilter, it is entirely feasible to construct the prisms and assemble some of the quilt top by machine. However, an alternative, quick assembly method, with machine-sewing throughout, is also offered here.

Read the Quiltmaking Basics and refer to them throughout. Remember that seam allowances must be added when cutting all pieces.

❖ **Preparing the Templates:** Make templates for the patches as follows: A is an 8 ½" (21.6 cm) square, B is the triangle that results from cutting A diagonally in half, C is the the triangle that results from cutting a 6" (15.2 cm) square diagonally in half, D is a 3" (7.6 cm) square,

E is the triangle that results from cutting D diagonally in half, and F is the triangle that results from cutting a 2 ⅞" (7.3 cm) square diagonally in half.

❖ **Cutting Borders:** From Fabric 6, cut 2 strips 3" x 64" (7.6 x 162.6 cm) and 2 strips 3" x 70" (7.6 x 177.8 cm) for the plain inner border. From Fabric 2, cut 2 strips 6" x 94" (15.2 x 238.8 cm) and 2 strips 9" x 70" (22.9 x 177.8 cm) for the plain outer border. Set these aside.

❖ **Cutting Patches:** From Fabric 1, cut 9 A, 4 B, 8 C, 24 E, and 42 F. From Fabric 2, cut 48 D and 112 E. From Fabric 3, cut 48 D, 144 E, and 42 F. Cut 40 E each from Fabrics 4 and 5.

If designing an original color arrangement, make a color key, and count up the number of same-lettered pieces to determine how many patches of each color are needed.

❖ **Assembling the Quilt Top:** Arrange all the patches according to the Quilt Top Diagram.

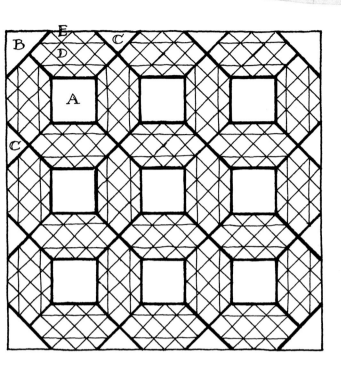

COLOR-IT-YOURSELF
QUILT TOP DIAGRAM

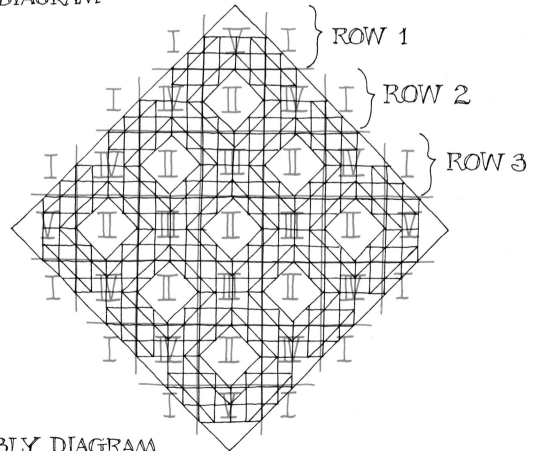

QUICK ASSEMBLY DIAGRAM

173

QUILT TOP DIAGRAM

FABRIC KEY   ▢ = FABRIC 3

■ = FABRIC 1   ▢ = FABRIC 4

■ = FABRIC 2   ▢ = FABRIC 5

I

II

III

IV

V

UNITS FOR QUICK ASSEMBLY

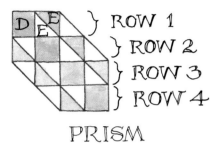

} ROW 1
} ROW 2
} ROW 3
} ROW 4

PRISM

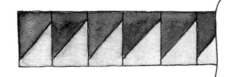

SAWTOOTH
BORDER

❖ **Hand-Piecing the Quilt Top (Prism Assembly):** Arrange the patches as shown in the diagram of the prism. Stitch the E patches together to form square units whenever possible. Stitch the patches and units together within each row, then stitch the rows together, taking care to match the seams. To assemble the quilt top, refer to the heavy lines on the Color-It-Yourself Diagram. Stitch the prisms and A squares into horizontal, then vertical rows. Hand-stitch the remaining seams. Add the corner B patches, and set in the C patches.

❖ **Machine-Piecing the Quilt Top (Quick Assembly):** Mentally set the quilt top on point, as shown in the Quick Assembly Diagram. The quilt is now divided into a series of blocks, rather than squares and prisms. Assemble each unit as follows, replacing the completed unit in the overall arrangement as you work:

Unit I (make 12): Stitch 2 E patches together to form a square; then add 1 E patch to 2 adjacent sides of the square as shown. The large triangle should have 2 sides 6" (15.2 cm) long and 1 side 8 ½" (21.6 cm) long, measuring within seam allowances.

Unit II (make 9): Stitch a Unit I to each side of an A patch. Each unit should measure 12" (30.5 cm) square within seam allowances.

Unit III (make 4): Stitch the E patches together to form square units. Stitch 2 square patches and 2 square units to form each square quadrant. Stitch the quadrants together in rows, then stitch rows together. Each unit should measure 12" (30.5 cm) square within seam allowances.

Unit IV (make 8): Assemble 3 square quadrants as in Unit III. Stitch 2 together, join a C patch to the third, then stitch the rows together.

Unit V (make 4): Assemble 2 square quadrants as in Unit III. Stitch them together, then join to the long edge of a B patch. Stitch the units into horizontal rows, then stitch the rows together, taking care to match all seams.

❖ **Making the Sawtooth Border:** Stitch F patches together in unmatched pairs to form 42 square units. Referring to the diagram, stitch 2 strips of 21 square units each, keeping the same fabric along each long edge. Stitch the strips to the top and bottom of the quilt top, placing the lighter fabric on the inside and easing each strip to fit.

❖ **Sewing the Inner Plain Border:** Using the narrow strips, stitch the shorter pieces to the top and bottom of the quilt top, and trim their ends even with the quilt top. Then stitch the longer pieces to the sides of the quilt top.

❖ **Making the Wide Plain Border:** Attach the wide strips in the same way as for the narrow border.

❖ **Assembling the Quilt:** Mark the quilt top for quilting if desired. Piece the backing, cut the batting, and baste the layers together.

❖ **Finishing:** Quilt as marked or as desired. In the quilt shown, patches are quilted ¼" (0.6 cm) inside their edges. Make a binding from Fabric 6 and attach it all around.

Cleaning, Repairing, and Storing Quilts

Museum-quality quilts should be cleaned and repaired by a textile expert. Most other quilts, unless they are very delicate, can be safely cleaned and repaired following a few simple guidelines. Any of the following three methods can be used to clean a quilt, depending on its fabric and condition:

❖ Dry Cleaning: All antique, silk, and wool quilts should be dry-cleaned by a firm experienced with old textiles and quilts. It may be necessary to consult a quilt expert in order to locate reliable cleaners.

❖ Vacuuming: The least stressful method of cleaning a quilt is with the soft brush attachment on a cannister vacuum cleaner. Lay the quilt flat on a clean sheet and cover it with a layer of light muslin, netting, or fiberglass screening. Gently vacuum the surface dirt from both sides.

❖ Washing: Most cotton and linen quilts can be washed. First, test for colorfastness by wetting a tiny area of each fabric type in the quilt and blotting them individually with paper toweling or white blotting paper to see if any dye adheres.

To hand wash, place the quilt in a clean bathtub half filled with a solution of warm water and gentle detergent. Agitate the water several minutes to loosen the dirt. Let the water drain out of the tub without removing the quilt. Rinse the quilt as many times as needed, drain, and press as much water as possible from it. Carefully lift it from the tub, and wrap it in thick towels to absorb more of the moisture. Do not hang a quilt over a clothesline to dry. Instead, lay the quilt on a clean sheet to straighten it, and let it dry flat. This is best done outdoors, though not in direct sunlight, with the quilt backing face up.

A quilt can be machine-washed on the gentle cycle only if the quilt is made from contemporary fabrics and is not valuable. Tumble-dry on a cool setting and remove promptly.

Quilt repair is dictated by the quilt. Very delicate or antique textiles should be repaired by a professional restorer. Call a museum or a well-known dealer for a recommendation. If a quilt is extremely damaged, however, it may be beyond repair, or it may cost more to repair than it is worth.

Hand-stitched quilts should be repaired by hand; machine quilts by machine, matching the original stitching as closely as possible. Fabric replacement should also come as close to the original as possible in content and style. Ripped seams are the most common type of repair and are fairly easy to correct.

The best way to store a quilt is flat on a bed. To store it folded, either in a cabinet or on display, fold the quilt in half and then in thirds, using acid-free tissue paper between all layers and between the quilt and the shelf. A cotton pillowcase makes a good protective cover if needed for storage. Every few months, refold them to prevent permanent crease marks and relieve pressure on the fabric. Quilts can also be wrapped around thick cardboard tubes (the kind used for carpets), though the fabric must also be protected from the cardboard and the shelf.

Always provide a stable environment for quilts: 50 percent humidity and temperatures between 60 and 70 degrees are ideal.

Nothing Goes to Waste~ Quilt Scraps

Decorating with quilt pieces has always been a warm-hearted way to brighten any home. Pillows, wall hangings, and tiny, touchable accessories can be made from old bed coverings and any bits and pieces left over from contemporary quiltmaking.

For example, it is a shame to discard an old, damaged quilt when it still has usable portions. Sturdy coverlets that are slightly worn can be recycled into cushions, table covers, dresser scarves, curtain valances, and bench covers. A creative eye might also envision small purses, stuffed animals, and toys.

So after determining it is not a valuable heirloom, do not be afraid to cut up a quilt that cannot be used as a whole. Quilts that are less than first class can also be used

Leftover fabrics and quilt patches can be stitched into heart-shaped pillows (above), then stuffed with fragrant pot-pourri. A quilted pillow cover, *too fragile for everyday use, is framed between wooden stocking stretchers (opposite).*

freely in rooms where a finer textile might not survive, such as a kitchen or bathroom.

Flea markets and yard sales are great places to search for less-than-perfect old quilts or quilt blocks. Be sure to explore bags or boxes; a sewing project, abandoned midway, might be hidden within. Whole counterpanes, torn or too worn to be used as is, may warrant a purchase if the price is right and the pattern or fabrics are appealing. Fragile pieces can be matted and framed under glass in the same way as a sampler or other handworked textiles.

Small quilts can easily be fashioned from a cache of squares, with the project completed faster than it would take to make a full-size quilt. Although small works are traditionally used as crib coverlets for a baby, they make cozy throws for sofas and chaises. They can also be effective wall hangings, especially in places where a large one would be overwhelming.

To try a hand at quilting without making an entire quilt, stitch a few blocks together, then use the pieces to

Pale blue-and-white patch-work pillows were newly made from squares of cotton fabric (left). The Bear Paw pillows were made from older quilt blocks. Chintz curtains soften the geometry of the quilts, providing a gentle backdrop. Pieced pillows (opposite) were fashioned from a combination of contemporary calicoes and vintage fabrics gathered at country fairs and auctions in Massachusetts.

decorate. Several blocks can make a snug tea cozy or a footstool cover. Balls are a favorite toy to make from scraps, which can also be folded lengthwise and seamed to make attractive curtain tiebacks. Older quilt scraps can be combined with newer fabrics. For example, it is easy to make a 26-inch square pillow, called a European sham, with old quilt blocks on one side and a new fabric backing on the other. Or an old block can be the centerpiece of a larger pillow made from newer fabrics.

Individual quilt blocks can be seamed along their outer edges to make pillows. Pieces that are truly antique can also be made into pillows; just be sure to set them in out-of-the-way corners where they will not be subject to much use. Very small pillows ~ about the size of an outstretched hand ~ look quite charming set in a chair where the back meets the seat. Fringed or tasseled ends accentuate their charm.

For the holidays, country Christmas stockings can be made from quilt scraps, sewn together in the familiar pattern and backed with felt or grosgrain. Patchwork and appliqué ornaments ~ angels, stars, Log Cabin diamonds ~ bring color and tradition to the tree.

A single block draped on top of a lampshade looks pretty with the light shining through it. A quilt piece is lovely under a glass plate that magnifies its details on a table. One wonderful square makes an impressive doily under a candleholder or vase. Another makes a potholder for the kitchen; just be sure to back it with fabric and fill it with batting for protection from the heat. Bibs for baby, placemats for the table, and thick, quilted trivets to set hot foods on are other ingenious ways to use quilt squares.

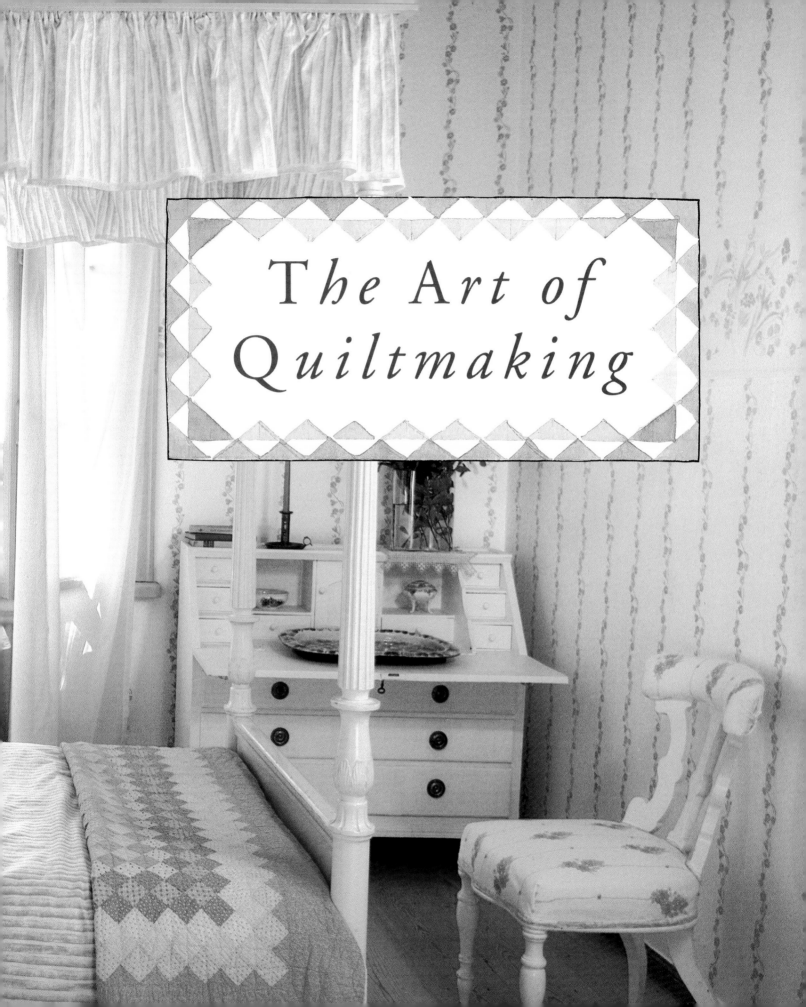

The Art of Quiltmaking

Quiltmaking Basics

The ultimate way to appreciate and enjoy quilts is by making one. Countless sewers have waded cautiously into quilting waters, starting with a pillow top or a quilted toy, and then found themselves so enamored of the art that they have gone on to make a whole quilt. Directions for twenty quilts, both patchwork and appliqué, of varying degrees of complexity, have been provided throughout the book. Here are the basic step-by-step instructions for making a quilt from start to finish.

❖ **Materials:** Unless you are making a novelty or Crazy quilt, select cotton fabrics 44"-45" (111.7-114.3 cm) wide. Closely woven but supple 100 percent cotton gives the best results. Wash cotton cloth to preshrink it and make sure it is colorfast; then iron it smooth.

❖ **Other Supplies:** You will need sewing and quilting thread, which traditionally are natural or black, although you may prefer to use matching or contrasting colors. Quilting thread is usually strong, 100 percent cotton (no. 50). A thimble is very helpful in hand-quilting, as is beeswax, which both strengthens the thread and makes it easier to pass through the cloth. Filler or batting is always optional, but it gives the quilt dimension and warmth. For the projects in this book, low-loft or traditional batting is recommended. It should be cut slightly larger than the size of the finished quilt. For tools, you may require many of the following: pencil; transparent, graphed ruler; yardstick; graph paper; tracing paper; cardboard; glue; dressmaker's marking pencil; scissors; sewing and quilting needles; pins; sewing machine (optional); steam iron.

❖ **Preparing Templates:** Outlines for templates are provided on pages 193-203, so you can mark stitching lines (not cutting lines) on your cloth. *Note that the templates are the size of the finished patch (the part that shows when the quilt top is assembled); be sure to read the section "Adding Seam Allowances" before you actually make them.*

To make these stiff patterns, draw the shape indicated in the directions on graph paper or trace the actual-size patterns on to tracing paper, leaving the seam allowance of your choice. Cut out the pattern piece, including any interior spaces. Glue the paper to a piece of cardboard, let the glue dry, then cut along the marked lines to complete the template. (You may use any stiff material other than cardboard, if you wish.) Test-fit templates together to check that adjacent pieces match. For small templates that you will use dozens of times, make several identical templates so you can replace them when the edges begin to fray.

❖ **Adding Seam Allowances:** *Seam allowances are not included in any patterns for templates or dimensions given for geometric shapes, so seam allowances must be added for all patchwork and traditional appliqué pieces.* This enables you to use whatever amount of seam allowance you wish, either the standard ¼" (0.6 cm) or ⅜" (1.0 cm), or even ½" (1.3 cm). When joining small patches, stitch ¼" or ⅜" from the edges, then trim the seam allowances to ⅛" (0.3 cm) to reduce bulk.

Everyone needs a room to call her own ~ especially a quilter, who must have space to spread out lots of fabric pieces. Inspiration seems to come more easily when the room is not just functional, but beautiful besides. This hobby room (opposite) was a living room; now the owner focuses on her quiltmaking at a cherry-top worktable that she designed herself. A patchwork

Trip Round the World quilt at the foot of this canopy bed (previous page) anchors a room decorated with contemporary fabrics and wallpapers ~ a combination of flowers, striped bed linens, and geometric patchwork designs. The quilt's pastel colors indicate that it was probably made after 1930, when pastel dyes and fabrics became popular.

❖ **Cutting and Making Backing, Borders, and Sashing Strips:** Before you begin cutting patches from a fabric, cut any of the larger pieces needed from the same fabric for backing, borders, and sashing strips. Make these pieces a little larger than necessary, in case your patchwork is off by a little. Note that dimensions of borders and sashing strips allow for extra leeway. It is easy to trim pieces down, but harder to solve a shortage problem attractively. Cut binding strips on the bias, twice the width of the desired finished binding [generally ⅜" to ⅝" (1.0 to 1.6 cm)] plus seam allowances. Cut blocks and patches from the remaining fabric pieces.

For backing twin-size and larger quilts, you may find larger widths of fabric (double cloth) in quilting stores; remember to preshrink this material. When working with standard-width fabric, you will need to piece several lengths together to obtain the necessary dimensions. Avoid a center seam; it is better to cut one piece in half lengthwise and stitch each half to the selvages of the other, full-width piece. Press the seams toward the center. The amount of standard-width fabric needed for backing is listed in the material requirements for each quilt.

❖ **Cutting Patches:** Lay the fabric out flat, wrong side up. Mark each patch, beginning with the largest template and proceeding to the smallest. Position each template on the fabric so as many straight sides as possible fall along the grain of the fabric. Use a sharp pencil (a light-colored dressmaker's marking pencil for dark fabrics) to draw around the template. For the next patch, reposition the template two seam allowance widths away and draw around it. *When you cut out each patch, be sure to leave a seam allowance all around.* If your quilt design is complex, it is helpful to keep identical patches (or patches designated for each block) in clear plastic bags.

❖ **Stitching Patchwork:** Patchwork may be hand- or machine-sewn. To join the patches, place two together, the right sides of the fabric facing and matching raw edges aligned. Stitch along the marked lines, continuing into the seam allowances unless otherwise indicated in the directions. For neat corners, match the seams, then pin through the seam at the point of the angle (on the marked stitching line) on both joined pieces. As you work, press the seams to one side, toward the darker fabric.

❖ **Making Appliqué Templates:** Make appliqué templates in the same manner as for patchwork, but be sure to place the template on the right side of the fabric, and draw around it with a pencil. Remember to leave space between each piece for a seam allowance [slightly less than ¼" (0.3 cm) is usually recommended]. Cut out the shape. Clip into the seam allowance almost to the marked line along any curves and inside angles. For outside angles, clip across the seam allowance, almost to the marked line, to reduce bulk. To help position a complex design, or several pieces, precisely, lightly pencil placement lines on the background fabric.

❖ **Working in Traditional Appliqué:** Determine the sequence in which pieces should be sewn down. Pin the pieces in place, overlapping them as required, and baste any small pieces. Use 18" (45.7 cm) strands of sewing thread and a small (#8 or #9), sharp needle. Knot one end. Turn under the seam allowance on the appliqué and match it to the drawing on the background, so both pencil lines are just hidden. Bring the needle from the wrong side of the appliqué out the front along the penciled outline, hiding the knot. Make very tiny overcast stitches as follows: Insert the needle down through the pencil line on the background fabric just beneath where you caught the foldline. Then bring the point back to the surface a short distance away and through the very edge of the fold. Pull the thread all the way through. Any clipped corners should be reinforced with two or three overcast stitches to keep them from raveling. If you plan on doing a lot of quilting, it is helpful to cut away any underlying appliqué fabric (preferably not the background) to avoid stitching through multiple layers.

❖ **Working in Contemporary Appliqué:** Iron the wrong side of the marked fabrics with a paper-backed fusible web (such as Wonder Under™ from Pellon). Set your iron temperature according to the manufacturer's instructions accompanying the fusible web. Cut out the

In a log house (above), one of the bedrooms is devoted to a favorite hobby – quilting. To ready the room for a quilting bee, comfortable chairs are drawn up to the frame. Years ago, the Bunny crib

quilt was a baby gift; now it is displayed on the wall. Rolls of cloth are stored in a basket in the corner; other sewing supplies are gathered on open shelves against the wall.

appliqué along the marked outline, *but do not add a seam allowance.* Peel off the paper backing and position the appliqué on the background. Iron to fuse it in place. Stitch around the appliqué over the raw edges; use a narrow, close, machine zigzag stitch, or work small blanket stitches by hand.

❖ **Assembling the Quilt Top:** Stitch the blocks or rows together in units as indicated in the quilt directions. Add any sashing strips (plain pieces in between the blocks). Trim the quilt top, if necessary, to square off the edges.

❖ **Attaching Borders:** First sew the border strips to the quilt, with an equal amount of cloth extending at each end. To miter the corners, lay the quilt top flat, right side

EMBROIDERY STITCH DETAILS

OUTLINE STITCH

BACKSTITCH

HERRINGBONE STITCH

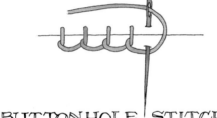

BUTTONHOLE STITCH

CROSS STITCH AND FRENCH KNOTS

SATIN STITCH

LAZY-DAISY STITCH

STRAIGHT STITCH

FEATHER STITCH

down. Hold adjacent ends of the border pieces together at the corners with right sides facing. Keeping the border flat, lift up the inner corners and pin the strips together diagonally from the inner corners outward on a 45 degree angle. Baste and then stitch on the basting line. Trim the excess fabric and press the seams open.

❖ **Preparing Backing and Batting:** Trim the edges of the backing 1" (2.5 cm) larger all around than the finished quilt top. Cut the batting (preferably low-loft or traditional) the same size as the backing. Place the backing, wrong side up, on a flat surface, and place the batting on top. Smooth these layers, then baste them together with very large basting stitches in a contrasting-color thread. Center the quilt top, right side up, on top. Smooth it, then baste. Start at the center each time and stitch outward to the midpoint of each side and to each corner. Also baste around the edges.

❖ **Hand-Quilting:** Mark the quilt top with any special quilting designs. For traditional designs, such as scrolls, chain links, wreaths, vines, and simple florals, you can find templates in quilting stores and patterns in books and magazines on quilting. Use water-erasable marking pens or dressmaker's tracing paper (like carbon paper) and a dull pencil.

In an Amish household, where mirrors and photographs are forbidden, a quilt can fill a room with color. Amish women work by daylight, gaslight, or candlelight, since their homes are without electricity. Abhoring waste, the quilters store up fabric that is left over from other family sewing and trade with friends for colors they need. On this Amish porch in Indiana (above), a Bow Ties quilt is in progress.

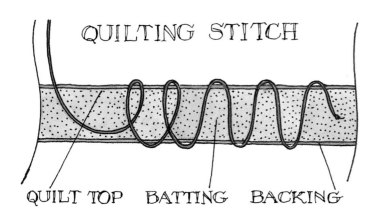

To quilt, work from the center of the quilt outward and stitch toward you. Turn the quilt as you progress, so you can work outward in all directions evenly. For best results, hand-quilt using a frame or hoop. Use strong quilting thread and a small (#8 or #9), sharp needle. To begin, thread the needle and knot one end. Insert the needle from the front 1" or 2" (2.5 or 5.1 cm) from where you wish to begin stitching, guiding it through the batting only and bringing it out at the beginning of a stitching line. Give the thread a little tug to pull the knot into the quilt top and leave it buried in the batting. Make running stitches through all layers. Most quilters prefer to use thimbles to push the needle through. Keep the index or third finger of your nonstitching hand underneath your work to feel the needle's point and to make sure it penetrates all layers. Make one stitch at a time or load several on to the needle before pulling the thread all the way through. It's not as important to make tiny stitches as it is to strive for even, consistent-looking stitches. When you reach the end of the thread or the end of a stitching line, end off: Make a tiny backstitch and reinsert the needle at the same place, bringing it through the batting only and then out on top, a few inches away. Clip the thread close to where it emerges.

❖ **Machine Quilting:** Use sewing thread and a straight stitch, 6 to 8 stitches per inch. Roll up half the quilt tightly and place this roll to the right of the machine needle; unroll it as you quilt toward the right. Reverse the quilt and quilt the left half in the same manner.

A standard practice is to quilt ⅛" (0.3 cm) beyond all the seams or around all the shapes you want emphasized. You may prefer to follow the marked lines of a quilting design, make parallel lines, or follow a grid. You can mark lines easily with strips of masking tape. Tape as you go; avoid leaving the tape in place, as the adhesive may cling when the tape is finally removed. For echo quilting, follow the contour of a patch or appliqué shape and work around it in increasingly larger, concentric shapes.

❖ **Tying or Tufting:** If you do not wish to quilt, you should still secure the layers to prevent them from shifting. You can do this by tying the quilt at regular intervals, such as at the intersections or the centers of the quilt blocks. Use pearl cotton, yarn, 6-strand embroidery floss, or ⅛" (0.3 cm) ribbon in a sharp embroidery needle.

For a conspicuous tie that adds a design element, begin on the quilt top. For an inconspicuous tie, begin on the backing. Insert the needle at the spot where you want the tie, and penetrate all the layers. Bring the needle back a

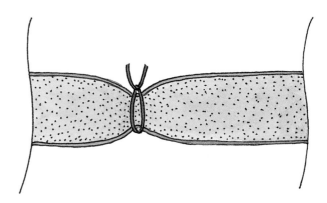

TYING OR TUFTING A QUILT

scant ⅛" away from where you began. Cut the thread ends 2" (5.1 cm) long. Knot the ends in a tight, square knot, then trim the ends to 1" or 1 ½" (2.5 or 3.8 cm).

❖ **Binding:** Piece the strips together so the binding is more than long enough to go all around the quilt. Press the seam allowance to the wrong side on one long edge. Pin the other long edge to the quilt top; begin sewing at a corner, leaving the appropriate seam allowance, taking tucks to miter the other corners. Stitch all the way around. Trim and finish the end neatly. Turn the binding over toward the backing, pin the pressed edge to the backing, and slip-stitch it in place all around.

❖ **Signing and Dating Your Quilt:** Signing and dating a quilt is important for posterity. In his classic book *Patchwork*, Averil Colby cautions against the modesty of placing anonymous initials and the date on the back of a quilt. He believes the correct places are either on the center panel or on a border pattern, and a proper inscription should include the day, month, and year of finishing, and the full name of the worker.

So sign and date your handiwork. Future generations will appreciate your thoughtfulness and will cherish your work all the more, knowing whose skilled hands made their heirloom.

Plain, Geometric, and Fancy Borders

Adding a border, or several borders, to a quilt can easily change a simple design into a dramatic one and enlarge any quilt. Borders can serve as a frame for a Medallion or a Star pattern, giving the quilt a more finished look. Colorful or pieced borders can add interest to an otherwise plain quilt.

❖ **Plain Borders:** A plain band of color used all around a quilt can tie it together, providing a frame for a motif or a unifying color theme. Use several plain borders together, perhaps of different widths, to add stripes around a quilt. Or try a very wide border as a dramatic accent for a simple patchwork design.

❖ **Geometric Borders:** Squares, triangles, diamonds, and rectangles of fabric can be pieced together into long strips to make borders that are colorful and fanciful. Keep the border in scale with the motifs of the rest of the quilt top. Color can either harmonize or contrast, depending on the desired result. Fabrics can be solid or patterned, but often there is enough pattern in the quilt top so that a plain border offers some visual relief.

❖ **Fancy Borders:** Making a prairie point (sawtoothed) or scal-

loped border requires a bit more labor, but the results can be spectacular. To make a prairie point border, cut squares of fabric, fold diagonally, and then in half again to make small triangles. Arrange these triangles along the quilt edge, points toward the center of the quilt, overlapping slightly, and baste into position. Fold the quilt edge so the triangles now face out from the quilt edge and the basting line is covered, and slip-stitch all along the edge of the quilt top. Turn the backing under and slip-stitch it along the seam. For a scalloped border, use the same procedure, but instead create U-shaped

pieces. Cut two identical semicircles of fabric, and seam along the curved edge on the wrong side; then clip and turn right side out for each scallop. Place prairie points or scallops side by side or overlapping along the quilt edges.

❖ **Other Finishes:** It is also possible to finish a quilt edge using cording, piping, braiding, or, for a luxurious Crazy quilt, fancy fringe or tassels. Soft cording now comes in various thicknesses to edge pillows or other small projects. Thick cording can also be useful if visual weight is wanted, especially if a quilt will be used on a bed rather than on a wall.

Pattern Pieces

The following pages contain unusually shaped pattern pieces needed to make quilts in this book. Each of the pieces is labeled with the name of the corresponding quilt and the pages on which the directions appear.

Please note that all the pattern pieces in this section must be enlarged to include the seam allowance of your choice.

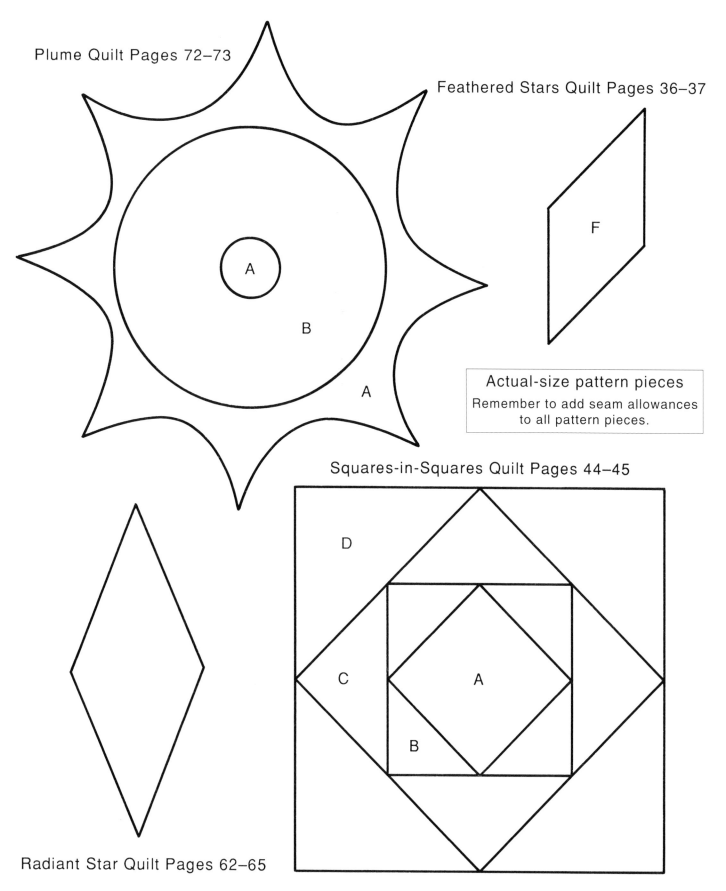

Plume Quilt Pages 72–73

Feathered Stars Quilt Pages 36–37

F

Actual-size pattern pieces
Remember to add seam allowances
to all pattern pieces.

A

B

A

Squares-in-Squares Quilt Pages 44–45

D

C

A

B

Radiant Star Quilt Pages 62–65

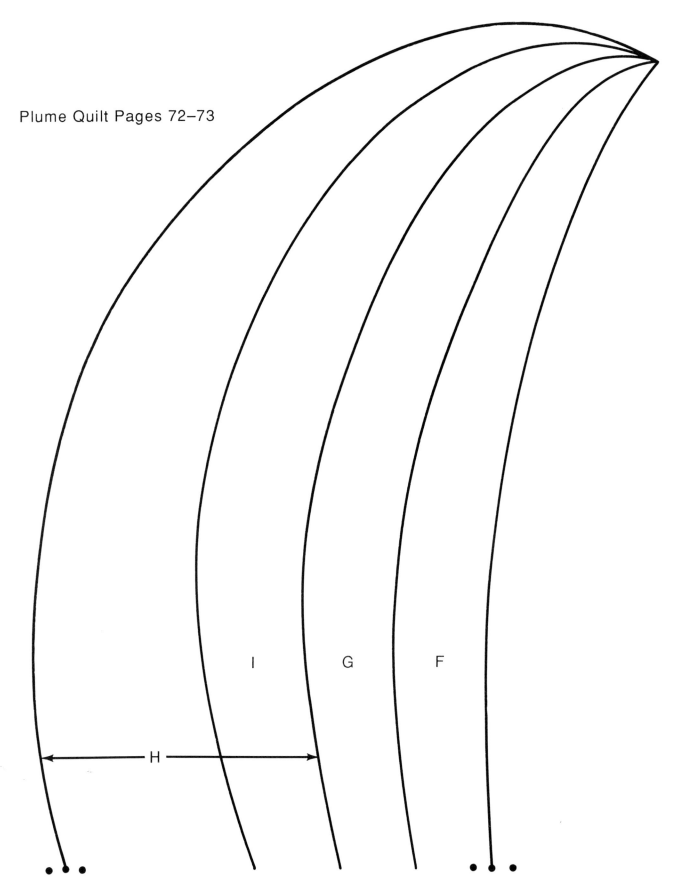

Plume Quilt Pages 72–73

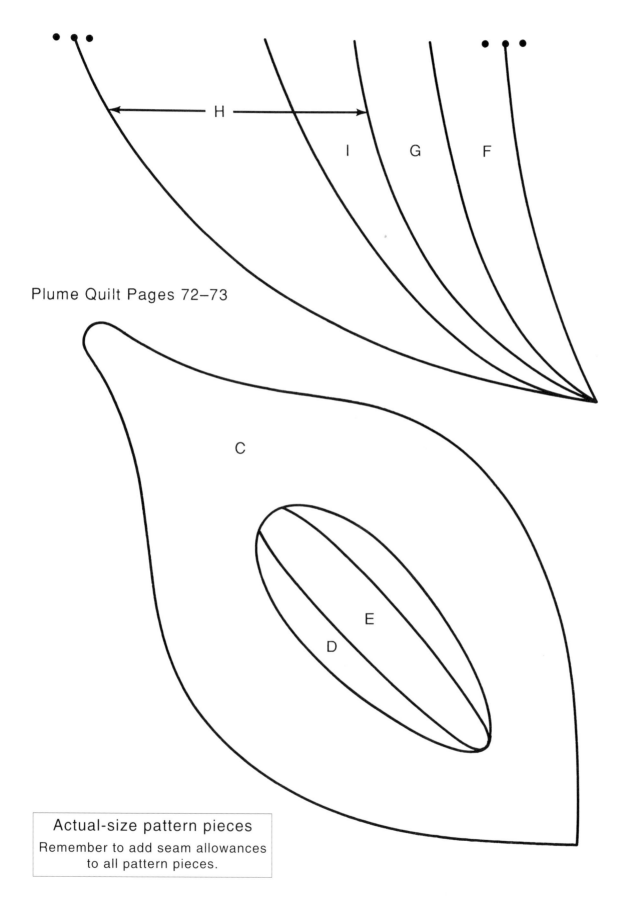

H

I   G   F

Plume Quilt Pages 72–73

C

E

D

Actual-size pattern pieces
Remember to add seam allowances
to all pattern pieces.

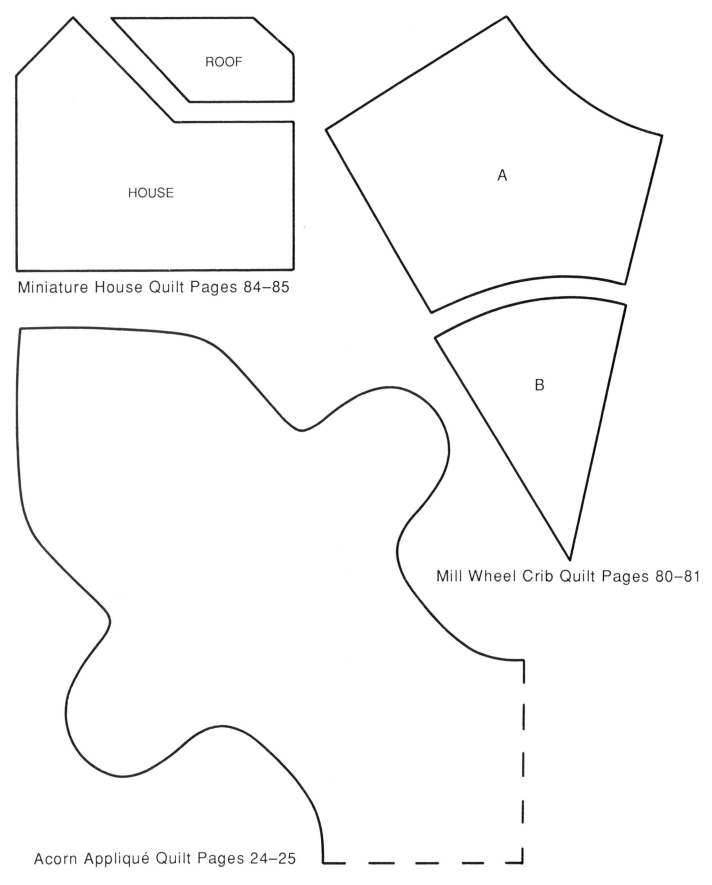

ROOF

HOUSE

Miniature House Quilt Pages 84–85

A

B

Mill Wheel Crib Quilt Pages 80–81

Acorn Appliqué Quilt Pages 24–25

Flower Basket Quilt Pages 102–105

Actual-size pattern pieces
Remember to add seam allowances
to all pattern pieces.

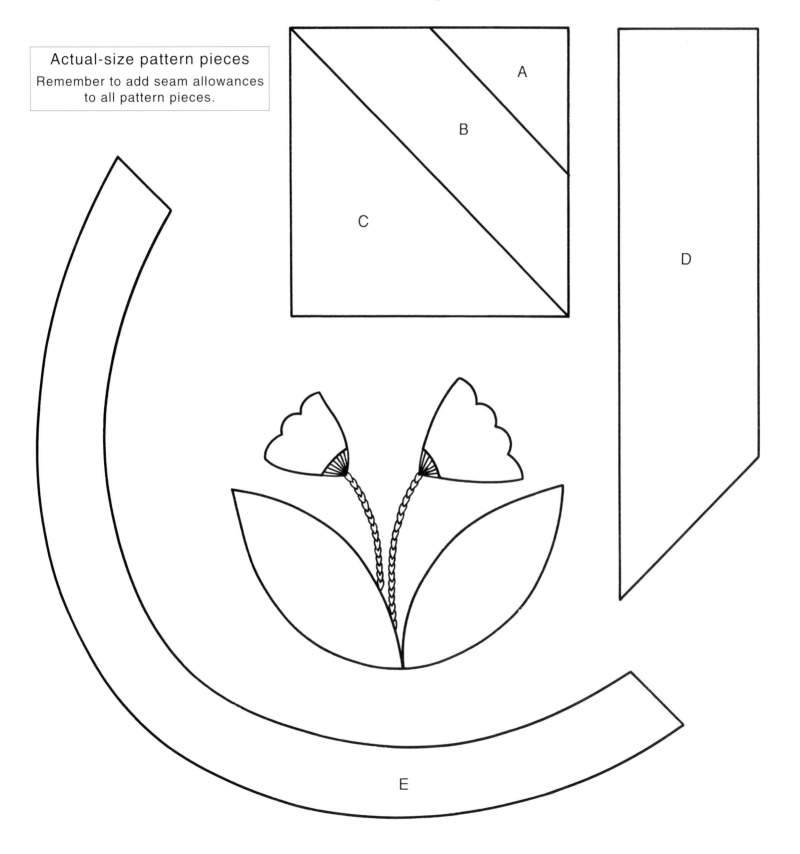

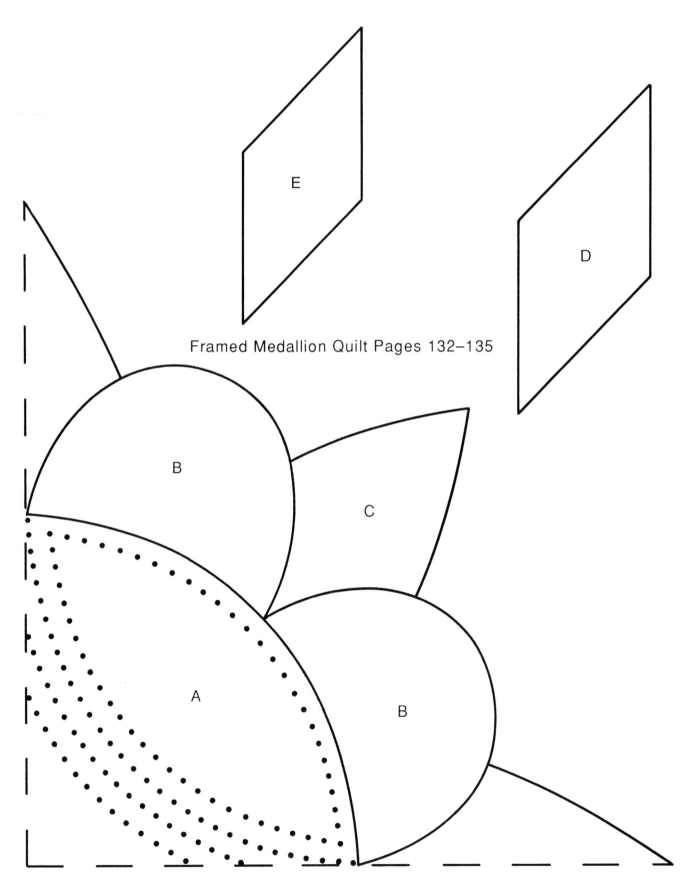

Framed Medallion Quilt Pages 132–135

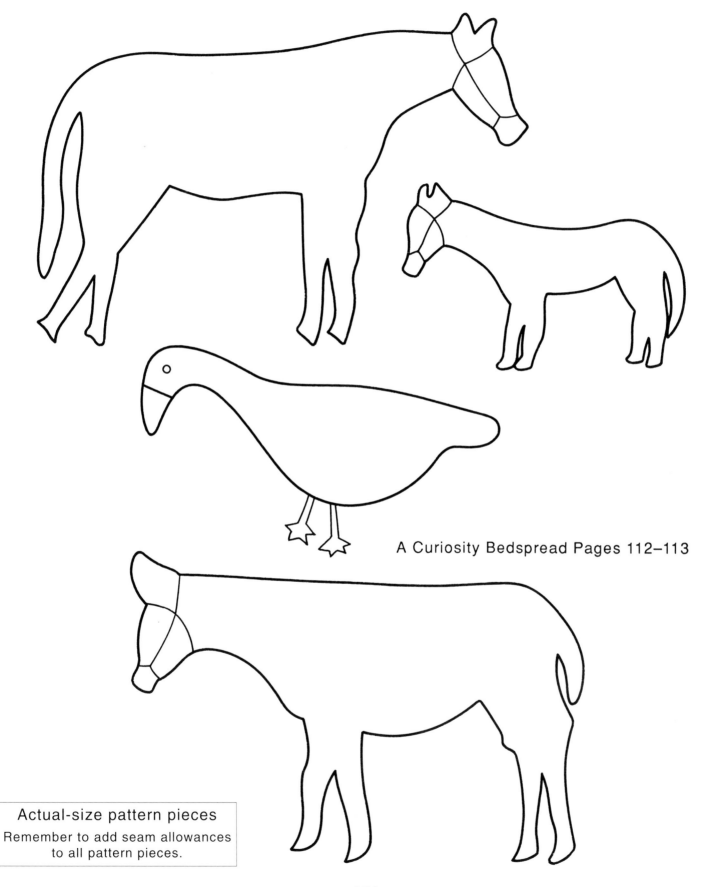

A Curiosity Bedspread Pages 112–113

Actual-size pattern pieces
Remember to add seam allowances
to all pattern pieces.

A Curiosity Bedspread Pages 112–113

A Curiosity Bedspread Pages 112–113

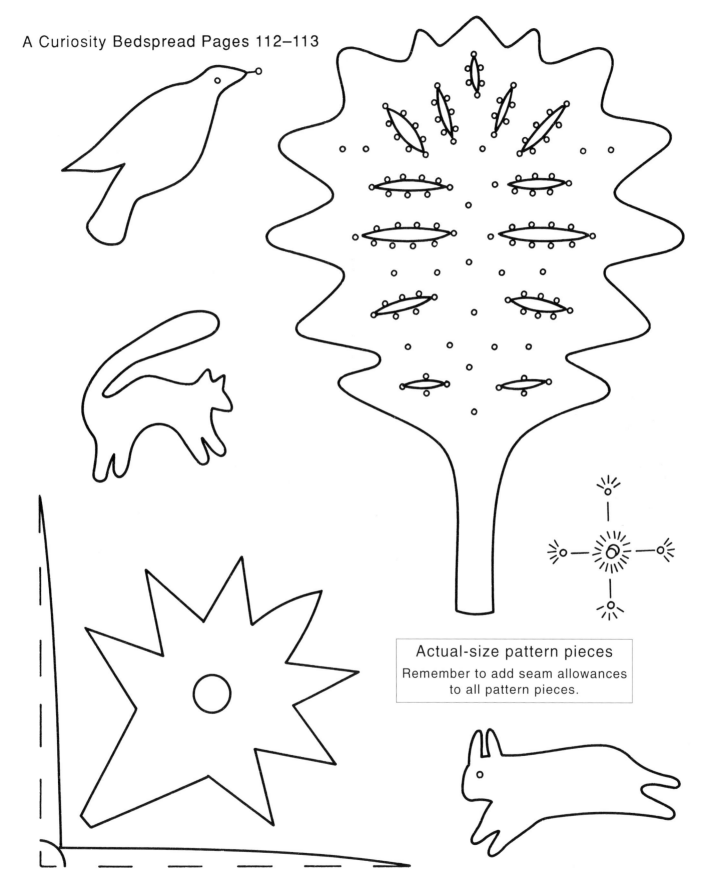

Actual-size pattern pieces
Remember to add seam allowances
to all pattern pieces.

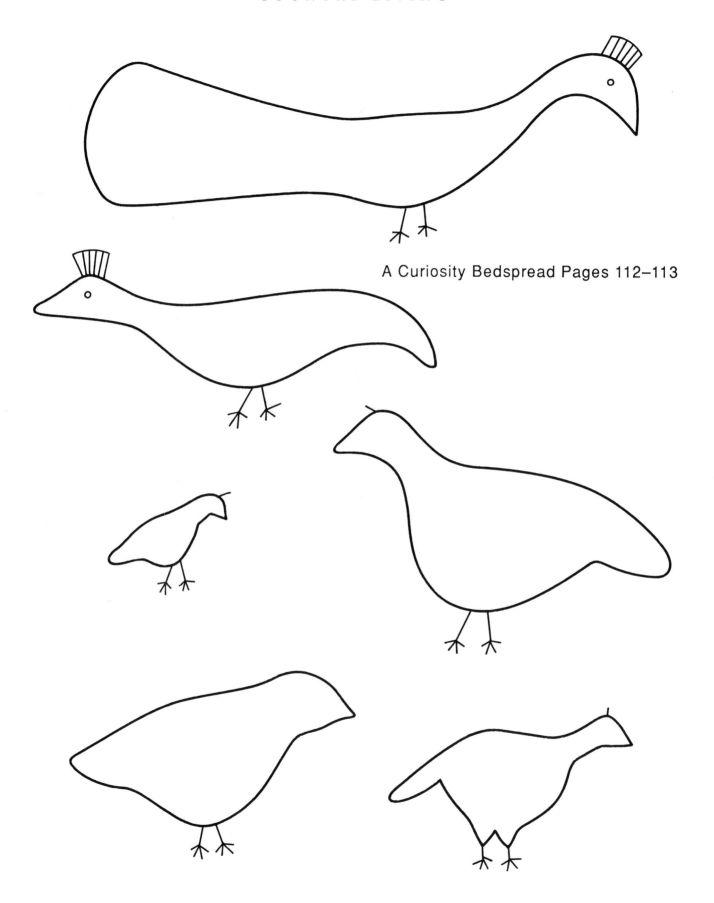

A Curiosity Bedspread Pages 112–113

Actual-size pattern pieces
Remember to add seam allowances
to all pattern pieces.

A Curiosity Bedspread Pages 112–113

Resources

Since a vast assortment of quilting resources are available in this country, we are able to list only a brief sampling here.

APPRAISERS

American Quilter's Society Certified Appraisers
P.O. Box 3290
Paducah, KY 42002

American Society of Appraisers
P.O. Box 17265
Washington, DC 20041

Appraisers Association of America
60 E. 42nd Street
New York, NY 10165

Fendelman & Schwartz
1248 Coast Road
Scarsdale, NY 10583

Lynda Peters
Winsor Road
N. Scituate, RI 02857

Joan K. Townsend
Oh Suzanna
16 South Broadway
Lebanon, OH 45036

Thos. K. Woodard
American Antiques & Quilts
799 Madison Avenue
New York, NY 10021

CUSTOM QUILTMAKERS

Freedom Quilting Bee
Box 43A, Route 1
Alberta, AL 36720
Will use your fabric or theirs; produce other quilted items as well

Mercer & Bratt Amish Quilts
P.O. Box 883601
San Francisco, CA 94188
Work with Amish crafters to custom-make quilts

FESTIVALS & FAIRS

American Quilter's Society Quilt Show and Contest
P.O. BOX 3290
Paducah, KY 42001
Large festival held the third or fourth week of April; includes auction, workshops, fashion show, vendors, quilt exhibitions, and show with prizes.

Creative Quilting and Fabric Art Festival
Ross Expositions
19 South B. Street, Suite 11
San Mateo, CA 94401
Over twenty small regional fairs.

The Great American Quilt Festival
61 West 62nd Street
New York, NY 10023
Five-day convention sponsored by The Museum of American Folk Art held biennially; includes several quilt exhibitions, lecture series, demonstrations, vendors, and workshops.

International Quilt Festival
14520 Memorial Drive #54
Houston, TX 77079
Largest quilt fair in the world held each fall; sponsored by the American International Quilters Association; features quilt exhibits, sales, vendors, and a quiltmaking academy.

The Mid-Atlantic Quilt Festival
6075 Route 202
New Hope, PA 18398
Four-day festival held in the last week of February in Williamsburg, Virginia; includes a themed competition with prizes, fashion show, quilt vendors, and workshops.

National Quilt Festival
Silver Dollar City, Inc.
Special Events Department
West Highway 76
Bronson, MO 65616
Two-week fair held in late August and early September includes quilt sale, competition with prizes, themed exhibition, vendors, and craftspeople.

The Pacific International Quilt Festival
P.O. Box 667
New Hope, PA 18398
Four-day fair held the first week of October in San Francisco; includes a themed competition with prizes, quilt exhibitions, fashion show, vendors, and workshops.

Quilt Celebration
15775 North Hillcrest, Suite 508-Box 304
Dallas, TX 75248
Large festival held the third weekend of March sponsored by the Quilters Guild of Dallas; features classes, vendors, quilt exhibits, and show with prizes.

A Quilters Gathering
Attn: Marie Gerary
P.O. Box 711
Westford, MA 01886
Four-day conference held the first week of November sponsored by the East Coast Quilters Alliance; includes workshops, lectures, vendors, contests, and invitational exposition.

Quilting by the Lake
P.O. Box 282
Cazenovia, NY 13035
Pair of four-day workshops held the last week of July and the first week of August; features all-day workshops and classes, special events, and vendors.

Quilt San Diego
P.O. Box 26902
San Diego, CA 92126
Biennual juried show organized around a theme; exhibits shown for several months in a museum setting.

MUSEUMS, ORGANIZATIONS, AND EDUCATIONAL STUDY CENTERS

The American International Quilt Association
14520 Memorial Drive #54
Houston, TX 77079

The American Quilt Research Center
Los Angeles County Museum of Art
5905 Wilshire Boulevard
Los Angeles, CA 90036

American Quilt Study Group
660 Mission Street, Suite 400
San Francisco, CA 94105

American Quilter's Society
P.O. Box 3290
Paducah, KY 42002

The Kentucky Quilt Project
P.O. Box 6251
Louisville, KY 40206

The Museum of American Folk Art
61 West 62nd Street
New York, NY 10023

Museum of the American Quilter's Society
P.O. Box 1540
215 Jefferson Street
Paducah, KY 42001

MAIL-ORDER SERVICES

Alaska Dyeworks
300 W. Swanson, No.101
Wasilla, Alaska 99687
Dyed fabrics

Cabin Fever Calicoes
P.O. Box 550106
Atlanta, GA 30355
Quilting supplies

Come Quilt With Me
3903 Avenue I
Brooklyn, NY 11210
Quilting supplies

HAPCO Products
46 Mapleview
Columbia, MO 65202
Quilting supplies

International Fabric Collection
5120 West Ridge Road
Erie, PA 16506
Imported fabrics

Keepsake Quilting
Route 25, P.O. Box 1618
Centre Harbor, NH 03226
Quilting supplies

Norwood
505 S. Division Avenue, Box 157
Fremont, MI 49142
Quilting frames

Osage County Quilt Factory
400 Walnut, Box 490
Overbrook, KS 66524
Quilting supplies

Pleasant Mountain Woodworks
510 Southgate Drive
Mt. Pleasant, TX 75455
Quilting frames

The Quilter's Sourcebook
The Vermont Patchworks
Box 229
Shrewbury, VT 05738
Quilting supplies

Quilting Books Unlimited
1911 W. Wilson Street
Batavia, IL 60510
Quilting books

The Stencil Company
P.O. Box 1218
Williamsville, NY 14221
Quilting stencils

Stitcher's Supply
125 50th Street, N.W.
Albuquerque, NM 87105
Frames and holders

Strings Attached
5250 Norfolk Street
Lima, OH 45806
Hand-dyed cottons

OTHER SUPPLIERS

The Bear's Paw
In the Canal Barn
Cedar Bay Road
Fayetteville, NY 13066
American handicrafts

Hinterberg Design Inc.
2100 Northwestern Avenue
West Bend, WI 53095
Quilting frames and hoops

Keepsake Quilting
P.O. Box 1618
Center Harbor, NH 03226
*Quilting patterns and
quilts, quilting stencils*

Quilts Unlimited
203 E. Washington Street
Lewisburg, WV 24901
Quilting supplies

Schoolhouse Quilt Shop
2872 Whipple Avenue
Canton, OH 44708
Quilting supplies

The Strawberry Patch Calico Shop
RD#3, Box 44
Columbia Cross Roads, PA 16914
Quilting fabrics and classes

PUBLICATIONS

American Quilter
Schroeder Publications
5801 Kenducky Dam Road
Paducah, KY 42001

Blanket Statements
American Quilt Study Group
660 Mission Street, Suite 400
San Francisco, CA 94105

Fiberarts
50 College Street
Asheville, NC 28801

The Quilter's Newsletter Magazine
6700 West 44th Avenue
Wheatridge, CO 80033

RESTORERS & CONSERVATORS

Jamar Textile Restoration Studio
250 Riverside Drive
New York, NY 10025
*Quilt and hooked rug restoration,
distributor of the Walker Systems
textile hanging devices*

Pilgrim/Roy Associates
5380 Shafter Avenue
Oakland, CA 94618
Quilt conservators and appraisers

Rocky Mountain Quilts
Gloria White
2 Ocean Avenue
Rockport, MA 01966
Quilt restoration

Rocky Mountain Quilts
Betsey Telford
3847 Highway 6 & 24 Alternate
Palisade, CO 81526
Quilt restoration

The Textile Conservation Workshop, Inc.
Main Street
South Salem, NY 10590
Conservation and preservation laboratory

VINTAGE QUILTS

American Antiques & Quilts
799 Madison Avenue
New York, NY 10021

Laura Fisher/Antique Quilts & Americana
1050 Second Avenue
Gallery 57
New York, NY 10027

Oh Suzanna
16 South Broadway
Lebanon, OH 45036

Shelly Zegart Quilts
12-Z River Hill Road
Louisville, KY 40207

Photography Credits

2 ....Keith Scott Morton
4-5 ....Keith Scott Morton
8 ....Keith Scott Morton
11 ....Keith Scott Morton
12-13........Keith Scott Morton
14 ....Jessie Walker
15 ....Keith Scott Morton
16 ....Keith Scott Morton
17 ....Jessie Walker
20-21........Keith Scott Morton
22 ....Jessie Walker
23 ....Keith Scott Morton
25 ....Keith Scott Morton
26-27........Keith Scott Morton (all)
28 ....Keith Scott Morton
30 ....Keith Scott Morton (above)
30 ....Jessie Walker (below)
31 ....Elyse Lewin
32-33........Jessie Walker
35 ....Keith Scott Morton
36 ....Joshua Greene
38 ....Jessie Walker
39 ....Paul Kopelow
42 ....Jessie Walker
43 ....Jessie Walker
45 ....Keith Scott Morton
46-47........Jessie Walker
49 ....Jessie Walker
50 ....Ralph Bogertman
52 ....Keith Scott Morton
53 ....Lynn Karlin (above)
53 ....James Levin (below)
56 ....Keith Scott Morton
57 ....André Gillardin (above)
57 ....Keith Scott Morton (below)
60 ....Jon Elliott
61 ....Jessie Walker
66 ....Keith Scott Morton

67 ....Keith Scott Morton
68 ....Keith Scott Morton
69 ....Ben Rosenthal
70 ....Michael Dunne
71 ....Jessie Walker (both)
74 ....Ralph Bogertman
75 ....Paul Kopelow
76 ....Keith Scott Morton
78 ....Keith Scott Morton
79 ....Paul Kopelow
82 ....Jon Elliott
83 ....Jessie Walker
84 ....Paul Kopelow
86 ....Jessie Walker
88 ....Keith Scott Morton
89 ....Keith Scott Morton
90 ....Keith Scott Morton
91 ....André Gillardin
92-93........Keith Scott Morton
94-95........Jessie Walker
96 ....Ralph Bogertman
97 ....Keith Scott Morton
99 ....Keith Scott Morton
100 ....Jessie Walker
101 ....Paul Kopelow
103 ....André Gillardin
106 ....Paul Kopelow (above)
106 ....Jessie Walker (below)
108 ....Paul Kopelow
109 ....Lilo Raymond
110 ....Keith Scott Morton
113 ....Paul Kopelow
114-115....Joshua Greene
116..........Lilo Raymond
118 ....Keith Scott Morton
120 ....Keith Scott Morton
121 ....Jessie Walker (above)
121 ....Jon Elliott (above)
124 ....Paul Kopelow
126..........Jessie Walker

127 ....Jessie Walker
128 ....Jessie Walker (both)
129 ....Keith Scott Morton
130-131....Keith Scott Morton
135 ....Paul Kopelow
136 ....Jessie Walker
138 ....Keith Scott Morton (left)
138 ....Jessie Walker (right)
139 ....Paul Kopelow
140 ....James Levin
141 ....Keith Scott Morton
142 ....Keith Scott Morton
143 ....Keith Scott Morton
144 ....Jessie Walker
146 ....Paul Kopelow
147 ....Paul Kopelow
148-149....Keith Scott Morton
150-151....Keith Scott Morton
152 ....Paul Kopelow
154 ....Paul Kopelow
155 ....Keith Scott Morton
156-157....George Ross
158 ....Jessie Walker
159 ....Keith Scott Morton
160 ....Jessie Walker
162-163 ...Paul Kopelow
164-165....Peter Vitale
166-167....Paul Kopelow
170 ....George Ross
171 ....Jessie Walker
177 ....André Gillardin
178 ....Jessie Walker
179 ....Joshua Greene
180 ....Lilo Raymond
181 ....James Levin
182-183....Keith Scott Morton
184 ....Keith Scott Morton
187 ....Keith Scott Morton
189 ....Jessie Walker